Chinese Furniture

CRAIG CLUNAS

Chinese Furniture

Photographed by Ian Thomas

VICTORIA AND ALBERT MUSEUM · FAR EASTERN SERIES

First published 1988 by Bamboo Publishing Ltd, London

Re-issued by V&A Publications, London, 1997

Reprinted 1999

V&A Publications
160 Brompton Road
London SW3 1HW

ISBN 1-85177-239-1

A catalogue record for this book is available from the British Library

Typeset by Dorchester Typesetting Group Ltd
Printed in Hong Kong

Contents

Note on Spelling and Pronunciation

The *pinyin* system of romanizing the Chinese script is used throughout, following the spelling given in *Xinhua Zidian*, revised edition (Peking, 1971). The only exceptions are Chinese terms and proper names within quotations, and the place names Peking, Canton and Hong Kong. Since no agreed standard exists governing word division in romanized Chinese, the grouping of characters has been left to individual authors to carry out as seems appropriate in individual cases.

The following few hints may help the reader unfamiliar with the system at least to pronounce words to themselves:

Initial *zh-*, as English *j-*
Initial *x-*, as English *s-*
Initial *c-*, as English *ts-*
Initial *q-*, as English *ch-*

Introduction

This book takes as its starting point the group of pieces of Chinese furniture which has been assembled over the years by bequest, gift or purchase in the Victoria and Albert Museum. At over seventy pieces, it forms one of the larger collections outside China itself. These individual tables, chairs and cupboards, long divorced from the context and the culture in which they were made, could potentially act as the stimulus to many kinds of investigation. In the light of our expanding knowledge about pre-modern China's material culture, anyone who undertakes to write about such artefacts has to tread a path between the contrasting and comparing of actual pieces, which risks descending into a culturally uniformed and vapid connoisseurship, and the erection of vast but flimsy hypotheses about Chinese society which leap unconvincingly from the particular to the too general. No leap is more dangerous or more seductive than that from 'understanding' an artefact to 'understanding' the society which produced it, though its perils seem not to have troubled many western writers on what have been termed the 'decorative arts' of China.

In the final chapter I have tried to show how the very term 'Chinese furniture' is not something self evident, a passive given from which investigation proceeds, but is rather a construct of the investigator. Thus I feel no apologies are required for the necessarily uneven coverage of certain topics. In any case, as I will argue in Chapter 3, the loss of whole classes of material, principally the plain lacquered furniture so prominent in early handbooks on taste, subverts from the beginning any attempt to construct a 'comprehensive' book on a neutral 'Chinese furniture'. The text which follows attempts to stress above all how Chinese furniture was *used*. Obviously in China as in the West luxurious items acted as carriers of social meaning and as markers of social status, but this status was not simply inherent in the timber or method of construction or even the form and decoration of the individual object. It resided as much in the deployment of objects within an interior (and occasionally exterior) setting showing a socially acceptable degree of taste and refinement, and in the ascribed social status of the objects' owner. The reader will therefore find here less about the timbers and types of joints involved in the manufacture of furniture (a subject which has been admirably treated by other writers) than about what types of object could acceptably stand where at what periods. The evidence is distinctly patchy. It is all too easy to seize on the statements of our few main sources and perhaps give them too much descriptive weight. However the study of European interior decoration has had rich and useful repercussions on the way furniture historians view individual objects, and it is hoped that a broader focus here may similarly aid future studies of types or even single pieces of Chinese furniture.

The text is laid out in a way which alternates chapters on a particular class of furniture, such as that for sitting on, with more general topics such as materials and workshop methods. The aim is to show in some measure the unity of the general theme with the particular piece. The great majority of the Museum's examples of Chinese furniture is here illustrated and discussed, the exceptions being pieces made to western designs for export, as well as a small number of fakes and very badly damaged objects.

All present and many past members of the Far Eastern Department have helped with the preparation of this book. I have also benefited greatly from the opinions and writings of Robert Ellsworth, Nick Grindley, Charles Saumarez Smith, Laurence Sickman, Nick Umney and Frances Wood. Professor Glen Dudbridge provided invaluable bibliographical instruction.

Sources for the Study of Chinese Furniture

To anyone familiar with the textual sources for the study of European furniture, and aware of the great advances which a knowledge of primary source material has brought in the last thirty years, the evidence for an investigation of China's furniture tradition may seem thin. There is not a single piece of Chinese furniture of any type or period signed by its maker. Indeed the vast majority of these makers are totally anonymous. There are no surviving account books, or collections of engraved design. There do not appear to survive even individual working sketches or models (if such things ever existed at all). The number of precisely and securely dated lacquer objects is small, and for hardwood furniture the number falls to single figures. However the supposed silence of the Chinese literary record on the subject has been overplayed by western authors. Contemporary evidence is available, from the viewpoint of both customer and maker, for perhaps the most interesting period of the development of Chinese furniture, the century between about 1580 and about 1680. This evidence may be difficult to interpret, but it can be used to shed light on the nature of the craft and on the perceptions of the Chinese élite as to how furniture ought to be. It cannot be used to assign a less nebulous date to individual unprovenanced pieces.

All pre-modern Chinese writers on furniture, in a display of literary piety, draw attention to a unique early monograph on one rather idiosyncratic type of table. This text, the *Yan ji tu* ('Illustrations of the Banqueting Board'), carries a preface dated AD 1194. Attributed to one Huang Changrui, it is in fact a set of instructions for arranging seven tables of three different shapes so as to form a variety of configurations suitable for various arrangements of guests. Of the tables themselves we learn nothing. The text was however well-known to later writers as the earliest mention of banqueting arrangements to be found in an independent form. A conscious imitation and expansion of it, using tables of more complex polygonal shapes, was completed in 1617.[1] The age in which it was written was one when, for whatever reasons, China saw a considerable expansion in the writing of what might loosely be called 'guides to elegant living'. The tone of these works is lapidary, allusive and high-handed. Things are never spelled out, the reader is presumed to be already 'in the know' about the topic under discussion, whether it be fashions in incense or clothing, styles in gardening or flower arranging, or types of desk accoutrement. Furniture is treated in the same manner. The highest praise offered is *ya* 'elegant', the most damning condemnation, *su* 'vulgar'. These are working translations only, of difficult terms which contain within them resonances of moral and social, as well as aesthetic judgement (if indeed any pre-modern Chinese aesthetic judgement could be said to be divorced from the social standards of the élite). No explicit criteria for *ya* and *su* are laid out, and any reader today has the additional obstacle that the nuances of fashion and taste on which they are based are often so slight as to be inscrutable to us across the centuries. These are in every sense prescriptive sources. They do not pretend simply to describe a situation, but to dictate an ideal, a fact which must continually be borne in mind when evaluating the very valuable evidence for material culture which they contain. Perhaps the most often quoted and influential of these cultural arbiters is the writer Gao Lian, whose *Zun sheng ba jian* ('Eight Discourses on the Art of Living') has prefaces dated 1591.[2] He has little to say on furniture, though, and is of less use to the present study than is Tu Long, whose *Kao pan yu shi* ('Random Notes of a Scholar in Seclusion') was completed in 1607.[3] Several of the latter's individual entries on couches and chairs were expanded in the single most important text for the study of upper-class attitudes to furniture in China around the year 1620. This is the *Zhang wu zhi* ('Treatise on Superfluous Things') by Wen Zhenheng (1585–1645).[4] Wen was a cultural, social and perhaps a political leader of the élite in the lower Yangtze-valley city of Suzhou, a city synonymous then as now with luxury craft production and a refined enjoyment of life. He held his position by virtue not only of his own talents in the esteemed arts of calligraphy, poetry and music, but of his descent from a line of notable scholars, artists and high government officials.[5] He embodied in his own person the heightened sensibilities of the late Ming man of wealth and taste, with his haughty contempt for everything he chooses to deem 'vulgar'. Not that he was a lone eccentric. Wen Zhenheng's writing on taste is given authority by his wide circle of contacts with other members of the élite who shared his tastes. We are reading in him the authentic voice of his class at his time. The fact that he borrowed from and extended the work of his slightly older contemporary Tu Long itself speaks for the existence of a consensus on style and design.

The *Treatise on Superfluous Things* includes twenty short but highly valuable sections on different types of furniture suitable for the elegant interior. As far as Wen Zhenheng was concerned, furniture was more than a necessary adjunct to civilized living, it was part of a continuous moral and aesthetic discourse (which ran through many other aspects of Ming culture) about the difference between *gu* 'antique' and *jin* 'modern', where *gu* does not simply mean 'chronologically old' but implies 'morally ennobling'. The evidence of numerous entries in his text proves that a piece of furniture made the previous day could be 'antique' if it fitted his standards correctly. He opens his chapter devoted to furniture with these words:

> 'When the men of old made tables and couches, although the length and width were not standard, when placed in a studio or room they were invariably antique, elegant and delightful. Whether sitting, lying or leaning back there was no way in which they were not convenient. In moments of pleasant relaxation, they would spread out classics and histories on them, examine paintings and calligraphy, display ancient bronzes, dine or take a nap – all these were possible. The men of today make them in a manner which merely prefers carved and painted decoration to delight the vulgar eye, while the antique pieces are cast aside, causing one to sigh in deep regret.'[6]

We are in a world where style, far from being a frivolous matter, is one of considerable importance. We are with an author who is situated firmly within the most advanced social and aesthetic circles of his day.

His major successor as a prescriptive writer on taste in furniture was a much more eccentric figure. Li Yu (1611–1680?) was variously a dramatist, a theatrical impresario, a novelist (and putative author of the pornographic *Prayer Mat of Flesh*) and a publisher as well as a theorist on horticulture and interior design. His *Xian qing ou ji* ('Random Notes on Times of Leisure')[7] of 1671 contains a quantity of material on furniture, much of it concerning ingenious devices of his own contriving which may never have commanded widespread acceptance. It is also a valuable source for attitudes to craftsmen, with some interesting light to shed on the relationship between maker and customer. Li Yu represents the end of the tradition of prescriptive handbooks of taste, which does not seem to have held much interest in the changed intellectual climate following the change of ruling house in 1644. It may have seemed to those who had lived through the catastrophe and bloodshed of the Manchu conquest to evoke too much the introspection, lack of application and sheer *dolce far niente* of the late Ming élite, one of the perceived causes of their downfall.

One further prescriptive source, but one written this time from the maker's point of view, is of great use. This is the *Lu Ban jing jiang jia jing* ('The Classic of Lu Ban and the Craftsman's Mirror'), named after the mythical patron of the carpenter's craft. The major part of the text as we now have it deals with rules for architectural woodworking.[8]

However the extremely rare edition dating from the Wanli reign (1573–1620) of the Ming dynasty, with its precious woodblock-printed illustrations, contains material on the making of furniture. This material is unique in affording a glimpse of the perceptions of the craftsman. It is, however, no plain and simple 'do it yourself' guide to Ming furniture making practice. The text is extremely corrupt, and considerable emendation has been necessary before a comprehensible version could be produced by the labours of the Chinese scholar Wang Shixiang.[9] It would be impossible for even the most skilled of cabinetmakers today to take tools and timber and produce a piece of furniture, by following the directions of the *Classic of Lu Ban* alone. The clue to the work's true status lies in its title. It is a *jing*, a 'classic', on a par with the classic texts underpinning the various ideological systems of Confucianism, Taoism and Buddhism. It is *meant* to be arcane and hard to interpret; it is meant to be the timeless, secret inner teachings of the carpenter's art, not a mundane guide to practical action, which was transmitted orally and learned by experience. Other specialists – doctors, physiognomists, geomancers, exorcists – had their 'classic' and carpenters should have one too.[10] Nonetheless, and totally thanks to Wang Shixiang's interpretative achievement, the text can be made to yield worthwhile material, which will be noted in the relevant sections below.

The descriptive literary record for the study of Chinese furniture is at once much larger and much more various than the type of text discussed above. Much of it is contained in a class of literature called *suibi*, literally 'following the (inclination of the) writing brush'. These collections of notes on topics of historical, literary or artistic interest, not excluding tales of the supernatural or simply interesting occurrences brought to the writer's attention, were an important mode of cultural expression for the male élite of Ming and Qing China. While aiming to give an impression of effortless ease, they are often quite carefully structured, and frequently feature sections on material culture (such as types of tea, styles of clothing etc.). They treat furniture, if at all, in passing, though this casualness can paradoxically increase the value of their testimony.

The inventory, a staple tool of research into the pre-modern western interior, is practically unknown in China. However one major inventory does survive, in the form of a record made of the property of the politician Yan Song, following its confiscation by the state on his fall from power in 1562.[11] Other inventories of state confiscations exist in manuscript form in the archives of the National Palace Museum, Taipei, though these remain unpublished and untapped by researchers.[12] The numerous catalogues of painting collections and of collections of other kinds of art object which have come down to us from Ming and Qing times hardly ever mention items of furniture, though this omission of itself tells us something about its status as a craft.

Imaginative literature is frequently more informative, and three works in particular give a rich and rounded picture of life in the mansions of the wealthy (if not always the tasteful). For the sixteenth century we have *The Golden Lotus*, and for the seventeenth *A Marriage to Astonish the Age*, both of which are anonymous works. For the eighteenth century we have Cao Xueqin's panoramic *Hong lou meng*, *The Dream of the Red Chamber* or *A Dream of Red Mansions*, now better-known to English-language readers through David Hawkes' masterly translation as *The Story of the Stone*. These three great novels, only a small fraction of the fiction written in China from the sixteenth to the nineteenth centuries, are nonetheless detailed enough by themselves to shed light on the lavish interiors they describe.

1 *Woodblock illustration* from the drama *Xi xiang ji*, 'The West Chamber', Nanjing edition, Wanli period (1573–1620).

These interiors are portrayed not only in words in Chinese literature, but also in the woodblock illustrations which frequently accompanied works of fiction, drama and poetry from at least the fourteenth century. These illustrations, it should be stressed at the outset, are of limited use in fixing secure dates to individual objects. The degree of detail which they contain is often too little to show whether the pieces depicted are of plain wood or of lacquered wood (though at least one western writer has chosen to assume they invariably show hardwood furniture). Their value can lie only in loose parameters for the dating of major stylistic groups, and more immediately in the information they can provide on the *use* made of furniture, its disposition in the interior. An illustrator working on a drama set in the remote past might perhaps introduce what he thought of as archaising features into the delineation of individual items. However, given the meticulous attention paid in book illustration to the niceties of social interaction (where the deployment of furniture played a major role) he was unlikely to substitute something meaningless to his readers for the arrangements of chairs and tables with which they were familiar. Hence the use made in this study of book illustration is to describe furniture in its social context, and in particular to point up the fluid arrangements actually pertaining, which contrast so strikingly with the formal, symmetrical arrangements laid down in the prescriptive sources[13] and accepted by some western commentators as inviolate. Something of the same use can be made of painting, with the added problem that the decline in the esteem enjoyed by figure painting and genre subjects was marked from the thirteenth century at least, leading to a disinclination on the part of major artists to paint scenes in which furniture figured prominently. The very conscious use made of the past when painting in this field meant that much of what was executed

showed its subjects seated on the ground in the manner common prior to the eighth century.

One body of comparative material not available to the western furniture historian, but increasingly plentiful in China, is that of excavated tomb models. In common with many other cultures, pre-modern China believed that goods included in the tomb of the deceased, whether in real or simulated form, would be enjoyed by them after death. Hence real jewellery, clothes and small personal items of the early and mid-imperial periods are among the finds of China's thriving archaeological profession. Furniture was generally represented
2 in graves by models of ceramic or wood. These can be of the greatest value, though it once again must be born in mind that no inferences can be drawn about the material of the furniture they represent. Wooden models may stand for lacquered wood, since it is for example certain that no real Chinese furniture was green, despite the prevalence of lead-glazed earthenware models of this colour. The results of individual excavations will be noted below.

The major, and overwhelmingly the most important body of evidence for the course of development of Chinese furniture lies with the surviving objects themselves, and it is to these that we now turn.

Seat Furniture

The Origins of the Chinese Chair

The still mysterious transition in living arrangements through which, by about the year AD 1000, the Chinese élite abandoned the indigenous East Asian seating posture of kneeling on the floor of a room in favour of high chairs from which the legs hang down has been the subject of several studies. These have been carried out by both Chinese and western writers.[14] The meagre literary and even more meagre representational evidence for this transition has now been worked over until it seems unlikely to yield further information, and has in fact been the basis for interpretations which are at times diametrically opposed. On some points there appears to be general agreement. All writers pick up the reference in the *Book of the Later Han (Hou Han shu)* to the dissolute emperor Ling Di (r.AD 168–189), and his taste for what among other eccentricities are described as *hu chuang* and *hu zuo*, though the interpretation of these terms is controversial. The word *hu*, the dictionary meaning of which is 'barbarian', has been used at various times to denote many peoples to the west and north of China. In some texts it can mean 'Indian'. It could mean the oases states of Central Asia, with their heavily Indianized cultures. It could refer to the nomadic peoples of the inner Asian plateau. What it certainly means is 'non-Chinese', and there is thus no escaping the conclusion that whether a *hu chuang* is a 'barbarian bed' or a 'nomad seat', whether a *hu zuo* is a 'barbarian chair' or a 'foreign way of sitting', some perceived foreign association was implied by the terms in the first centuries of the Christian era.

Certainly the Chinese were in contact with peoples using what we would recognize as 'chairs' from at least the fourth-third centuries BC. One piece of material evidence which has been largely overlooked is a representation of a backed, fixed-frame chair on which sits a deity or a figure of authority, on a felt hanging excavated from the tomb of a nomad in the Altai region of Siberia.[15] The Altai peoples possessed Chinese luxuries. The trade routes which brought such goods may have brought some of the nomads' cultural traits back to China.

In the centuries following the fall of the Han dynasty in AD 220, the flavour of an alien and unfamiliar culture clings to any form of raised platform seating, whether folding (as the *hu chuang*) or fixed frame. It clings also to the manner of sitting with the legs hanging down. In the middle of the fifth century, ambassadors from

15

southern China to the ethnically non-Han Chinese court of the Nan Qi dynasty at Luoyang were still surprised at the habit of sitting in this manner during formal audiences.[16] This posture, associated as it was with representations in religious art of the future Baddha Maitreya, and with the significant 'other' of the threatening northerner, was a more major rupture with Chinese tradition than was the use of the high-platform seat. This at least had a formal relationship to the early Chinese mat-platform, in its basic meaning that to be raised off the floor (to whatever height) meant to be raised in status. It is this change in posture, not the change in the item of furniture, which leads to the situation in which China, alone among east Asian cultures, developed high furniture in pre-modern times.

Additional evidence for such a view can be found in pre-modern Japan, where in this as in other matters the culture patterns of early China were preserved. The woven-seated, raised thrones of Buddhist religious leaders, on which meditation was practised, were transferred to Japan along with much of the ritual of religious observance. They are frequently depicted in the sculpted and painted portraits of these hierarchs.[17] However, the squatting posture remained the norm there, the secular chair never developed. Japanese draughts may be every bit as chill as those of China, but the fact that raised seating in secular contexts never gained currency suggests that it was more than purely practical considerations which led to its adoption on the mainland.

Chinese monks of the fifth, sixth and seventh centuries used high platforms with woven seats.[18] By the end of this period high seating was in use in semi-lay contexts. A mural of seventh or eighth century date shows diners at a religious feast seated with their legs hanging below them, on long benches. Another mural, from a tomb dated AD 756 shows what is clearly a high-backed chair, on which the tomb's occupant sits in what one might now begin to call the modern Chinese manner.[19] By the years around AD 840, not only were chairs being represented on the walls of relatively modest tombs, they were available both in monasteries, where it was polite to offer one to lay visitors, and in government offices in the provinces, where they were the common seating platforms of members of the secular élite.[20]

A growing body of archaeological evidence would support the view that the two centuries between about 900 and 1100 saw the triumph of the chair, and of its necessary corollary, the high table. Not only murals, but miniature tomb models, and even full-size though flimsy pieces have been excavated.[21] These wooden replicas of furniture are of greater value than any two-dimensional representation, but it would still be unwise to rely too much on them. In particular they are a poor guide to constructional details, since they are not designed to bear the loads of full-size pieces. However they are revealing about the major stylistic currents of woodworking, and disquieting in that they show numerous types of object to have existed many centuries before the earliest surviving example. The earliest extant actual pieces of furniture, a chair and a table from a site in Henan province, datable by inscription to AD 1104, share this feature. Though both pieces are now in extremely poor condition, enough remains in particular of the table to point up its striking resemblance to tables such as those shown in plates 28 and 30.[22] The extremely slow moving 'classic' style seems to have established itself very early, a fact which cannot but render most attempts at a precise framework of dating for this material well nigh impossible.

In the tenth century, floor sitting was still practised in intimate contexts. When the second emperor of the Song dynasty, Taizong (r.976–997) visited the house of his late father's respected prime minister the fact that they took wine together on the floor was already rare enough to be worthy of note.[23] By the twelfth century it could no longer be assumed that gentlemen would know how to comport themselves elegantly in this fashion, necessitating an essay on the subject by the philosopher Zhu Xi (1130–1200) for use by his students.[24] The choice of this by now archaic pattern of sitting was a deliberate element in a revival of classical manners and morality. Sitting on a mat on the floor remained a part of mourning ritual into the late imperial period, but the chair was now here to stay for almost all domestic contexts.

Armchairs of the Ming and Qing

The earliest surviving Chinese chairs represent, however, a late point in the form's development, almost none being earlier than the Ming period (1368–1644). From the last century of that period, the late sixteenth and early seventeenth centuries, come several pieces in the Museum's collection which embody many of the features of the classic 'Ming chair'. None do this better than a pair of armchairs in *huali* wood, of striking modernity in the simplicity and balance of their lines.

3   In the Chinese terminology of today these are *guan mao shi yi*, 'official hat-shaped chairs'[25], the name deriving from a supposed resemblance between the square backs, with the top horizontal rail protruding over the back posts, and the winged hats which were part of the formal dress of Ming officials. The term is not seen in Ming texts, where chairs of these proportions are called *chan yi* 'meditation chairs' by the *Classic of Lu Ban*.[26] However Gao Lian, writing in 1591, describes a 'meditation chair' thus:

3 *Pair of armchairs*, *huali* wood. About 1550–
1600, height 104 cm, height of seat 50 cm,
length of seat 61.5 cm, FE.54 & 55–1977,
Given by Sir John Addis.

'A meditation chair is half as big again as an ordinary chair. Only the "water polish" ones are fine, though speckled bamboo is also possible. In this style the horizontal rail for pillowing the head at the top of the back needs to be broad and thick before they are acceptable for use.'[27]

In the early 1620s Wen Zhenheng was to write of a 'meditation chair' as being simply a type of seat made from naturally gnarled timbers. This rustic furniture is not represented in the V&A collection, though known from numerous pictorial representations as well as surviving objects. Wen dismisses as 'a vulgar pattern' the 'meditation chairs of Zhuanzhu lane' (a street in Suzhou), confirming that there were at least two contemporary views of what a chair of this name should look like. He also reveals that, 'although the styles for chairs are very numerous . . . in general low is better than high and wide better than narrow.'[28]

The present pair are far from being half as big again as the majority of Ming chairs, but they do conform in proportion to the specifications given in the *Classic of Lu Ban*. The joinery which they embody is a fine example of the art as it developed in China. Only four pieces of wood are used for the four verticals of the front legs and front arm-posts, rear legs and back posts, with each vertical passing through the frame of the seat. This frame, in one of the most pervasive elements of the constructional language employed in Chinese cabinetmaking, is formed from four pieces of wood which are mitred (i.e. touch at a 45° angle) together at the corners. The tenons (integral pins) on the long sides of the frame, which here form the back and front of the seat, fit into mortises (holes) on the short sides. Typically, these mortises are cut right through the wood of the short sides, so that the tenons are exposed. In this case they are clearly visible as darker rectangles of wood on the sides of the seat. Many other tenons are exposed too, as for example the tenon affixing each arm to the vertical post, again visible as a rectangle of darker wood.

The exposure of tenons has been advanced as a feature of significance in the dating of Chinese hardwood furniture. It does certainly seem to be the case that Chinese furniture from the fifteenth to nineteenth centuries underwent a process whereby the technical expedients involved in holding a piece together became less evident. This involved a distancing in some cases from the techniques of architectural wood-working. Some arguably very early chairs show tenons which are not merely exposed flush with another surface, but which actually protrude a little way beyond it,[29] an early and entirely unconscious expression of Piet Mondrian's theory of space, '. . . where

4 *Detail* of FE.54–1977, showing exposed tenon on the rear of vertical post.

lines cross or touch tangentially but do not cease to continue.'[30] A progression from protruding tenons, through tenons exposed but flush to tenons concealed within 'blind' mortises is certainly plausible. However it has little explicatory force as a means of precise dating, being too all-encompassing. The presence of exposed tenons on objects known to be of mid-nineteenth century date should alert us to the dangers of converting this feature into some sort of touchstone.

Another technical feature which may possibly be of greater value is the observed seat configuration of both chairs in this pair. The underside of the seat frame clearly shows holes drilled in all four sides, presumably to sustain a woven seat of some heavy fibre. However the seats are at present solid. A board, supported by two transverse braces, in turn supports fine woven bamboo matting. It is clear that the arrangement of the seats has been altered at some time in the chairs' history. Robert Ellsworth has asserted that all chairs made prior to the eighteenth century show evidence of originally having had such a soft, upholstered seat of woven matting.[31] It is certainly the case that chairs for which an early date is claimed do generally show evidence of drilled holes in the underside of the seat frame, while pieces clearly of the nineteenth century do not. Nevertheless the date and extent of the complete revolution in seating construction which has been argued remains a matter of speculation.

Grounds for dating these chairs to the late Ming period are to be found in graphic sources, as well as excavated models of similarly proportioned (though far from identical) chairs from tombs of the 1590s and 1610s.[32] These are, in fact, rather unusual in the concave finishing applied to all the members, perhaps as a means of mitigating the severe angularity of the basic profile. This way of treating the surface of the wood is also seen on a famous canopied bed in the collection of the Nelson-Atkins Museum, Kansas City, although there it is only the outward surfaces of the members which are concave. The curves given to the arms and top rail also have a balancing effect, if occasioning a considerable wastage of timber. This is also the case with the curve of the splat, or backrest. The curved splat, whether simply concave or, as here, worked in the S-curve is a feature which is not only aesthetically satisfying but is ergonomically effective in increasing the comfort of the sitter.[33] It is seen in Chinese furniture several centuries before it makes its first appearance in Europe.

How were such chairs used? The very fact that they survive in pairs suggests of itself something of the symmetry ideally aimed for in Chinese room arrangements. Wen Zhenheng lays down a set of four chairs as being the most suitable arrangement for use in a gentleman's study.[34] However the real social situations revealed by illustrations to Ming and Qing fiction and drama show that actual configurations of

5 *Underside* of FE.54–1977.

5

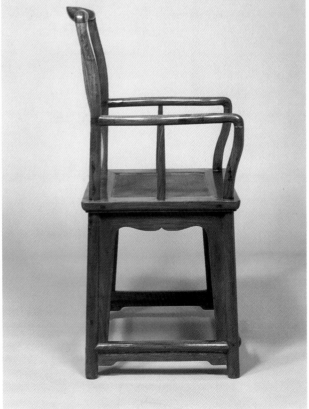

6 *Armchair*, *huali* wood. About 1550–1650,
height 104 cm, height of seat 50 cm,
length of seat 60 cm, FE.17–1980.

furniture within a room were not always as rigorously arranged about an axis as theory would suggest. Nor were individual pieces of furniture restricted to a single use. Book illustrations show 'official hat chairs' in use at the dinner table (though the form without arms may have been more common there), in the main hall of the house for the reception of guests, and at the writing table.[35]

A closely related type of chair, and an example close in date to the previous examples, is an armchair in *huali* wood, where the top rail does not protrude over the posts. Wang Shixiang calls this type a *nan guan mao yi* 'southern official hat chair', though whether 'southern' refers to the style of the chair or of the headgear is not made clear.[36] This too may be a 'meditation chair' in the slightly obscure terms of the *Classic of Lu Ban*. It is closely paralleled by a model in wood, actually of a chair within a closed sedan, from the tomb of a man who died in 1589.[37] The underside of the seat again shows traces of the holes drilled to carry soft webbing. More unusually several joints, those between the arms and the front and back posts, and between the back posts and the top rail, show a discolouration which reveals that these joints were once strengthened by metal straps. Whether these straps were original, or whether added later, and at what point they were removed, remains uncertain.

Such chairs shared the varied uses of the 'official hat armchair'. However it is worthwhile stressing that the vast majority of the population never sat on high chairs of this type, which have retained to this century in Chinese culture something of the connotations of status and authority with which their origins were associated. Even among the élite, the subordinate status of women meant that they rarely sat on chairs in mixed company, being restricted to stools unless they were venerable or important. Thus an illustration to the 1616 edition of *The Golden Lotus* shows only the central male character and his principal wife sitting on chairs to dine, while secondary wives and concubines sit on stools. Two incidents in the mid-seventeenth century novel, *A Marriage to Astonish the World* are revealing. The bullying and dissolute 'hero' is summonsed before a magistrate on a charge of having driven his wife to suicide. He has however bribed the functionaries so effectively that he is not treated like a criminal but like an honoured guest, and is even given 'a high-backed chair to sit on'. His concubine is sentenced to a term in prison, yet thanks to his money she lives a life of luxury inside. She is discovered in one scene sitting on 'a square scholar's chair', while a group of wardresses sits at her feet on low benches and stools.[38]

As in our own culture, inviting someone to sit was an important social gesture. When in 1678 an emperor wished to show particular

7 *Detail* of FE.17–1980, showing traces of metal fitting.

8 *Woodblock illustration* from the novel *Jin ping mei* 'The Golden Lotus', chapter 24, 1616 edition.

22

9 *Armchair, hongmu* wood. About 1700–1750, height 105 cm, height of seat, length of seat 57 cm, FE.2–1971.

grace and favour to the candidates in a special examination he offered them chairs at a banquet. This act of condescension, where stools were the most that could be expected, was well worth the attention of the chronicler.[39]

The plain hardwood furniture of the sixteenth and seventeenth centuries is of a quality which can mislead one into a total identification of this type of object with the Ming period. Yet the appearance and construction of furniture did not magically change with the change of ruling house in 1644. An interesting comparison with the chairs discussed above is afforded by an armchair in the timber now known in Chinese as *hongmu*, the decorative detailing of which suggests, by analogy with porcelain decoration in particular, a date in the early eighteenth century. Here, all the members have a circular cross section, and there is no exposure of constructional tenons. There is, though, evidence of the use of wooden pins to strengthen joints such as those between the back posts and top rail. There is also evidence on the underside that the conversion to a solid wooden seat is of very recent date, since the knotted palm fibres of the upholstery remain clearly visible. The single brace under the middle of the seat is also part of the original configuration, and is worked in a simple shallow curve to support the sitter's weight.

10 *Underside* of FE.2–1971.

23

Round-backed Armchairs

Chairs such as the above represent one major 'family' of classic Chinese furniture. A related family is formed by those chairs which surmount the basic seating platform with a curving superstructure forming a continuous support for the back and arms. In modern Chinese, these are *quan yi*, 'round chairs'.[40] Some Western writers have favoured the self-explanatory term 'horseshoe-back armchair'. In the sixteenth and seventeenth centuries, such chairs were, with the addition of two carrying poles, converted into light open sedan chairs, and it is in this guise, as the *ya jiao shi*, 'office sedan type' that they appear in the *Classic of Lu Ban*.[41] The Pan Yuncheng tomb of 1589 contains a model of just such a conveyance.[42] However, far from all round-backed chairs were originally intended for sedans. The existence of pairs again points to their use in formal room settings. Graphic sources show them in use for dining, and reveal that they were markers of high status, seats of honour. Whenever a representation of a banquet shows both round-backed and square-backed armchairs in use, it is the latter which are occupied by the more important guests.[43] They are seen too as the official seats of magistrates. In the late Ming period they bore the imposing name of *taishi yi*, 'Grand Tutor chairs'. A text of the early 1600s explains that, 'A chair with a curve that joins up and comes forward is called a Grand Tutor chair'.[44] This name was still current for a large armchair with a curving back in the late Qing period.[45] However it should not be applied too rigidly, as it has also been demonstrated that it is one which has over time referred to three different kinds of object. In the twelfth century it meant a folding chair with a curved back, in the sixteenth a fixed-frame chair with a curved back and in the eighteenth it could mean a particularly wide, but square-backed armchair.[46] Nevertheless the type seen here retained currency, and connotations of status, well beyond the Ming dynasty and was probably in production nearly into our own day. Miniature versions were made to seat clay portrait models of Danish merchants, brought back from China in 1732.[47] It is probably also significant that these were the seats preferred by the members of the governing élite when they came to have their photographs taken for the first time in the late nineteenth century.[48]

11   The individual curved-back armchair in the Museum's collection shows the form at its most typical. This is the form which was so immediately influential on the Danish designer Hans Wegner, inspiring (perhaps through the medium of the Copenhagen models) his *Kinastol*, 'Chinese chair' of 1944.[49] As with the square armchairs discussed above, the verticals of the legs and the posts supporting the arms are formed of single pieces of wood. The single curve of the back and

11 *Armchair, huali* wood. About 1550–1650, height 97 cm, height of seat 50.5 cm, length of seat 59 cm, FE.72–1983, Addis Bequest.

arms by contrast involves precise joinery of occasionally three but, more commonly as here, five pieces of timber. This is achieved by a joint variously described as a 'cogged scarf joint' or 'pressure peg joint' by western writers, in which each member is lapped over the other, with a ridge which fits into a groove cut across the diameter of the circle. A rectangular wood pin is then fitted in to force the two pieces apart and so firm up the joint. The difficulty of doing this accurately with two already curved pieces of wood suggests the possibility that the arm components may have been assembled before the final shaping when a rounding shave took place.

12   A pair of curved-back chairs are in most respects very close to the single chair. All three have at one time had drilled seat frames. All three show, as indeed do the square armchairs, considerable evidence of wear and tear on the bottom front rail, where the feet would have rested to raise them from the cold of the immediate floor level. The pair do though display a slightly different construction, with massiveness of effect sacrificed to ease of assembly. Here the front legs and the front arm posts are not continuous, the arms pulling back to enter the seat frame about 10 cm behind the legs. This 'pull-back' of the arms can be seen on the possibly early eighteenth century armchair above, but it would be unwise on such grounds alone to make this constructional feature a definite indicator of date.

12 *Pair of armchairs,* huali *wood.* About 1600–1700, height 98.3 cm, height of seat 51.5 cm, length of seat 59.3 cm, FE.66 & A–1983, Addis Bequest.

Folding Armchairs

The 'Grand Tutor chair', the fixed-frame chair with a curved back was descended from a form of more ancient folding chair. Such folding chairs did not go out of use in the Ming and Qing periods. Examples survive in both hardwood and lacquered wood. The Museum's collection includes a particularly important and lavishly decorated example of the latter, an imposingly large folding chair decorated with carved red lacquer on a wooden core. The carefully built-up layers of the hardened lacquer, whose red colour is achieved by the admixture of mercuric sulphide ('cinnabar'), are carved with patterns of writhing dragons among clouds in a style datable to around 1500.[50] The presence of five-clawed dragons so prominently in the decorative scheme raises the possibility that this piece was once at least intended for use in the imperial household. Certainly sixteenth century emperors when on their travels used such folding chairs. A Ming author who tells us that by this time in the early 1600s such chairs were known as 'Dongpo chairs' after the poet Su Dongpo (1036–1101) also reveals the flourishing trade in stolen pieces from the palace in Peking, including 'old items of carved lacquer', snapped up from under the noses of the uncomprehending locals by dealers from sophisticated southern Suzhou.[51] Hence it is perfectly possible that items such as this chair entered general circulation as antiques before this century.

13

14

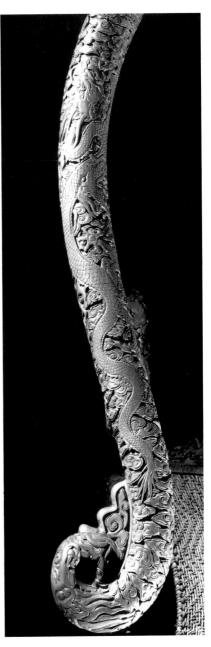

14 *Detail* of FE.8–1976, showing carving on arm.

13 *Folding armchair*, carved red lacquer on a wood core. About 1500, height 114.5 cm, height of seat 60 cm, length of seat 71.5 cm, FE.8–1976, Given by Sir Harry Garner and Lady Garner.

The folding chair, perhaps because of its connotations of antiquity, remained a rather grand seat throughout the sixteenth to eighteenth centuries. An eighteenth century emperor sits on one to receive the homage of central Asian tribesmen, in a celebrated painting by the court artist Giuseppe Castiglione.[52] Folding chairs appear regularly in 'ancestor portraits', the formal posthumous paintings necessary for family and clan cults.[53] An eighteenth century example decorated in painted gold on a red ground retains some of these associations of solemnity and grandeur. But a *jiao yi* 'folding chair' was also an article of convenience, its portability making it suitable for casual games of chess in the garden, and making it handy to have several around in the reception room of an expensive brothel for coping with an influx of honoured but unexpected guests.[54] Model folding chairs in the context of other furniture in a group of tombs of the mid-sixteenth century show that they too were used for dining.[55] The *jiao yi* was common enough to be the only kind of chair included in an illustrated child's primer of everyday objects published in 1436 and reprinted through the Ming period.[56]

15

Low Chairs, Stools, and Beds

The survival of fine hardwood furniture well past the middle of the seventeenth century is attested by a pair of low-backed armchairs in *huali* wood, of a type perhaps datable to the period c.1660–1720. This type has been called *meigui shi yi* 'rose type chairs' by modern writers, though it remains unclear how early this term came into use or exactly what it means. A confusion may be at work with the words *meiren yi* 'beautiful lady chair', since these more modest seats may have been intended for women.[57] They can be seen in early Qing book illustration and painting used in just this way.[58] An alternative explanation of the lowness of their backs is that they were designed to stand under windows, though this arrangement was explicitly condemned by Wen Zhenheng.[59] The seats of both chairs have been drilled, but several decorative features combine to suggest a date still in the early Qing. One is the upright angularity of the back, demanding a seating posture different from those allowed by the curved splats of earlier pieces. This alteration in body language is a major difference between the typical sixteenth century chair and the typical eighteenth or nineteenth century chair. Another is the eclectic mix of elements in the low-relief carved decoration. The apron under the seat, with its complex carving outline, carries interlocking floral scrolling very much in an earlier tradition. The back and arms show a more 'up-to-date' design of squared scrolling, ultimately derived from the very early metal and jade decorative tradition, the later manifestations of which have been labelled as 'archaistic'.

Similar scrolling can be seen on the sides of a square stool of late seventeenth or early eighteenth century date, where the scrolling is matched by a rigidification of the line of the apron. This no longer flows, but turns corners at a sharper angle. The piece however retains a curving, rather than a squared-off foot, and is drilled under the seat frame for the installation of a soft upholstered seat. The present hard mat seat is secured by strips which are in turn fixed into the frame of the top by wooden pins. The visual evidence for the ubiquity of stools, especially as seats for women, in Ming and Qing China is not matched by their presence in the Museum's holdings, this being the only example.

Two of the most important furniture types, with very early antecedents, were the *ta* or 'couch' and the *chuang* or 'bed'. The former in particular was of prime importance to the Ming writers on taste, who give this dominating feature of the private apartments pride of place, with copious detailed specifications.[60] From these often very plain pieces descend the ornate couches of the eighteenth and early nineteenth centuries, generally decorated in a variety of lacquering techniques. Those from the palaces of the aristocracy, able to tap the

16

17

18

19

20

17 *Woodblock illustration* from the drama *Huang qui feng* 'The Phoenix seeks a Mate', early Qing edition.

29

products of workshops under direct imperial control, deserve the name of 'throne', even if some of their owners lacked the power which such a word implies in English.

If the couch dominated the male study, then the canopied *chuang*, with its rich silk hangings, was a centre of life for the female members of rich families, the platform on which they spent much of their time. Both couches and beds had existed before the change to high seating from the eighth century and they remained surfaces on which people knelt or squatted, as well as reclined. A sixteenth century *da chuang* 'great bed', also known as a *ba bu chuang* 'eight paces bed' or *ta bu chuang* 'bed with a footstool' could be a massive structure, a room within a room with solid sides and an integral antechamber. A *liang chuang*, or 'cool bed', retained the antechambers but replaced the solid walls by textiles. The next step down was the *teng chuang* 'rattan bed' or *jiazi chuang* 'frame bed', without the antechamber.[61] At the time of writing, the Museum has only succeeded in adding to its collection a seventeenth century bed of this type, unfortunately too late for publication.[62] A much later 'rattan bed' of mid-nineteenth century date in the Museum is framed by a completely circular canopy. Made of wood richly inlaid with boxwood and ivory, it is decorated in a manner which the early western traveller Robert Fortune described in 1847 as being a speciality of the port city of Ningbo.[63] The full visual effect of such a bed is inseparable from its silk hangings, hangings to which the seventeenth century aesthete Li Yu devoted a great deal of thought. Sensibly pointing out that half-a-lifetime is spent in bed, he claims that not enough attention is paid to it. As well as inventing a method of installing a shelf for fresh flowers within the curtains, he claimed to have developed devices for keeping the curtains tightly closed, and for draping the curtains on a separate pyramidal framework over the framework of the bed itself, thus concealing the woodwork and preventing the trapping of mosquitoes on the inside.[64] His emphasis on hiding the actual bed frame should remind us that, in the Ming and early Qing at least, it was as likely to be the textiles which were the centre of decorative interest. The low survival rate of lacquered Ming furniture as against hardwood pieces, and the separation of furniture from textile hangings can lead us into a false dichotomy where 'Ming' equals 'plain' and 'Qing' equals 'ornate'. Certainly from the eighteenth century the focus of attention, and the chief field for adornment of a chair ceased to be the textile drapes and became the surface, usually lacquered, of the chair itself.

16 *Pair of low armchairs, huali* wood. About 1660–1720, height of seat 47.6 cm, length of seat 59 cm, FE.74 & A–1983, Addis Bequest.

18 *Stool, hongmu* wood. About 1680–1750, height 54.5 cm, seat 57.5 x 57.5 cm, FE.6–1979.

19 *Top* of FE.6–1979, showing wooden pinned retaining strips for mat seat.

20 *Throne*, painted lacquer on a wood core. About 1725–1750, height 135 cm, height of seat 60 cm, length of seat 141 cm, W.81–1923.

21 *Bed*, wood inlaid with ivory and boxwood. About 1850, height 212.2 cm, length 221 cm, width 122.5 cm, 495–1905.

Lacquered Chairs of the Qing Period

Various forms of painted lacquer predominated in the fine furniture industry from the eighteenth century. Painting in gold on black had been practised at Canton since the sixteenth century, probably under Japanese stimulus, and much furniture in this style was produced there for export to Europe from about 1720. Given this fact, it is tempting
22 to assign a mid-eighteenth century 'Grand Tutor chair' to a Canton workshop. A chair of almost identical pattern remains in the Palace Museum, Peking.[65] There are several distinctively 'Qing' features to this piece apart from the surface decoration. One is the vertical back, replacing the shaped back of earlier types. This angular form came to dominate in Chinese furniture just as the supposedly Chinese-inspired style of curving splat spread through the English furniture industry. In fact there is no evidence that furniture in the domestic taste was imported into eighteenth century Britain, and it was architectural detail as reproduced in books of illustrated ornament which formed much of the raw material for exoticizing design. Another feature seen on later Chinese furniture is the very wide seat.
23   Polychrome painted lacquer armchairs, both large and small, are also represented in the collection, datable by the parallels between their decorative schemes and those on ceramics, textiles and objects of other media. For the following century, the evidence of photography is
24 valuable for establishing the usage of and date of chairs, typically often lavishly inlaid with mother-of-pearl and openwork carving.

A taste for exoticism in the west, coupled with the gradual absorption of China into the world market for craft goods led to the manufacture from about 1860 of 'Chinese' furniture aimed at foreign markets. Pieces produced in Shanghai and Ningbo often incorporated panels of the intricate figurative domestic and temple woodwork associated with nearby Dongyang county. This may be the sort of
25 panel seen on the back of a particularly ill-proportioned armchair, elaborately carved and lacquered red all over in the Victorian impression of China. The back and arms are removable, perhaps for ease of packing and shipment as much for mobility within China.

Softwood Furniture

The majority of the furniture discussed above is luxury furniture, produced in specialist workshops for clients at the top end of the market. The vernacular furniture of Qing China, the fittings of more modest homes and often made of locally available softwood timbers,
26 are poorly represented. A chair and its accompanying stand of cypress (*Cupressus funebris Enth.*) were originally acquired by Kew Gardens in

22 *Armchair*, gold painted black lacquer on a wood core. About 1730–1800, height 102.5 cm, height of seat 51.5 cm, length of seat 67.1 cm, W.9–1931.

23 *Pair of low armchairs*, polychrome painted red lacquer on a wood core. About 1730–1800, height 80 cm, height of seat 49 cm length of seat 50 cm, W.83 & 84–1924.

26 *Chair and stand*, cypress wood. About 1880, height of chair 100 cm, height of seat 51.5 cm, length of seat 50 cm, height of stand 77 cm, FE.33 & 34–1970, Given by the Royal Botanic Gardens.

25 *Armchair*, lacquered and gilded wood. About 1880–1910, height 99 cm, height of seat 46.5 cm, length of seat 57.5 cm, FE.38–1970, Given by Brigadier Leslie H. Aste.

24 *Armchair*, one of a pair, polychrome painted lacquer on a wood core. About 1770–1820, height 96 cm, length of seat 61 cm, W.4–1955, Given by Mrs Van der Elst.

1886 as specimens of the wood, sent from the city of Ningbo. The hard wooden seat is typical of the chairs of this period, as is the squared scrolling under the seat and the low-relief carving on the three-panelled splat. The chair may once have formed part of a set, either of six or eight each with its attendant stand for teacup and spittoon, to be set in a reception hall at right angles to the back of the room in two facing rows.

The Materials of Chinese Furniture

From its crystallization in the Song period, the Chinese furniture tradition was represented by objects made of lacquered wood, which employed most of the techniques of the lacquerer's art, and by objects in which the surface of the timber was left undecorated or treated at the most by staining and polishing. The vast majority of the timbers used were from indigenous Chinese species of tree, something which remained the case into modern times. Although north China in particular has historically suffered from severe deforestation (wood being also a necessity in architecture and as a source of energy), locally grown wood has never been unobtainable. Of the one hundred and thirty-four species recognized as being native to the northern province of Hebei in the 1930s, no fewer than fifty-five were said to be in at least occasional use for the construction of furniture. These included not only unsurprising woods like oak, elm and maple, but also various types of chestnut, poplar and birch as well as occasionally mulberry, apple, pear and even the lacquer tree itself.[66]

There were, of course, marked regional variations across China. In the 1920s Rudolf Hommel noted that in the poorer mountain regions those who were not well off were forced to rely on bamboo (strictly speaking a grass, and not a timber) as a furniture material.[67] The sixteenth century writer Xie Zhaozhe, himself from the southwestern province of Fujian, drew a basic division between the fortunate southerners, who used fir for building, elm for furniture and *nan* wood (a species of the *Phoebe* genus) for coffins, while northerners were forced to rely on mulberry, willow, the Chinese scholar tree (*huai*) or pine. This meant that their furniture and utensils were, he condescendingly tells us, 'coarse and useless'.[68]

In Sichuan province the speciality timber for fine furniture was that of the Red Bean tree (*hong dou shu*), the botanical name of which, *Ormosia hosiei*, commemorates to this day the earnest British consular official who was the first person to describe it in a western language.[69] Some examples of particularly large tables in this timber were presented to the Yongzheng emperor in 1726 by the governor of Sichuan.[70]

Timber for furniture, as well as for building and other purposes, was an item of inter-regional trade. By the late eighteenth century at the latest, large commercial plantations existed whose occasionally rebellious workforces were a source of anxiety to the central government.[71] From the middle of the seventeenth century a centre of the timber trade had been Wuhan, the major commercial city on the

middle reaches of the Yangtze. Its excellent river communications made it a natural point for the valuable hardwood timbers of sub-tropical south-west China to enter the national market, and this trade in luxury wood eventually led to one in more common woods for building. It is however significant that, as with other types of trade in pre-modern China, it was expensive luxury goods which paved the way.[72]

It is on the luxurious, close-grained hardwoods used in Chinese furniture that most attention has focused. Robert Ellsworth has very sensibly advanced the view that, given the thicket of terminological confusion, in which the same species can have more than one Chinese name, more than one species share the same Chinese name, while neither botanical nor Chinese names fit one-for-one onto English names, the best solution is to retain the Chinese terms for general use.[73] This has been the approach adopted here. It has the advantage of concentrating on the visual appearance of the wood as perceived by the original makers and customers, since the application of the names does not appear to have changed much in pre-modern times. What was seen as *huali* wood in the sixteenth century was still seen as *huali* wood in the nineteenth. That does not mean that the material of individual objects cannot be identified with certainty in scientific terms, at least at the level of genus. It can, and individual identifications have been carried out by Jo Darrah of the Department of Conservation, V&A Museum. Her research would suggest that the general identification of *huali* wood with members of the genus *Pterocarpus* is correct, though it has not yet proved possible to be so certain about which species of this timber are involved. What is not now and never will be possible is a simple identification of one Chinese name with one English and one botanical name. The testing of a considerable body of hardwood furniture at the Philadelphia Museum of Art revealed that objects all made of a timber which the makers would have called *huali* were made either of a species of *Pterocarpus* (which a modern British cabinetmaker would call 'padouk') or of a species of *Dalbergia* (which would be a 'rosewood').[74] *Huali* wood is the timber most widely represented among the objects in the Museum's collection. It is a tropical hardwood, providing planks of a considerable size which are often richly grained. The colour can vary considerably, and it is the modern Chinese practice to reflect this by distinguishing between *huali* itself, *huang* 'yellow' *huali* and *lao* 'old' *huali*.[75] Such a distinction is not however seen in Ming and Qing written sources, where *huali* is used generically, and it is this practice which will be followed here. The different names do indeed reflect variations of tone or grain, but it must be kept in mind that these can be the result of surface treatment, or even of different methods of cutting the same log, as well as from a differentiation of species.[76]

27

Where did *huali* wood come from? It was available both within the boundaries of the empire and from abroad, from south-east Asia. One fourteenth century source describes it as coming from 'the Southern Barbarian Region',[77] while a text of the 1520s records it as a product of what are now southern Vietnam and Thailand.[78] However one of the major sources of supply was within China, albeit an area on the very periphery of Chinese culture. This was the island of Hainan off China's extreme south coast, inhabited by several ethnically distinct peoples of whom the Li were and remain the most numerous. One Ming writer states, '*Huali* wood, chicken-wing wood and sappan wood are all produced in the mountains of the Li. To obtain them, one must deal through the Li people, since outsiders do not know the paths and cannot find them, and since the Li tribes would not allow them to.'[79]

To the early twentieth century encyclopaedist Xu Ke *huali* wood was still to be found on Hainan island, though the monopoly of the Li tribes had been broken. He adds the information (not necessarily correct information) that this expensive wood has a swirling grain if taken from an old tree, but a straight grain if taken from a young tree.[80] As recently as 1957 Chinese botanists have coined the Latin name *Dalbergia hainanensis* to cover one at least of the hardwoods from this botanically rich island.[81]

The absence of any explicit mention of *huali* wood from Ming and Qing texts on overseas trade such as *Dong xi yang kao* ('An Investigation of the Eastern and Western Oceans') may reflect a perception that most of the sources were within the empire. It may on the other hand reflect a low level of trade, or a lack of interest in timber as an object of commerce. Non-Chinese sources are slightly more forthcoming. As early as the sixteenth century Portuguese ships were paying their anchorage dues at Canton in 'Brazil wood'.[82] Certainly Thai merchants brought tropical timber to Canton in the seventeenth and eighteenth centuries.[83] European merchants too were involved in the luxury timber trade. In 1775 the five ships of the English East India Company to visit Canton in that year brought with them over 270 tons of 'redwood' (though this may in fact have been sappan wood, used as dyestuff)[84], while in the early eighteenth century European merchants regularly shipped small quantities of *zitan*, a much prized purplish-brown timber which was also used for fine furniture.[85] All sources agree that *zitan* was an imported timber, and correspondingly precious. Considerable quantities of it were stockpiled in the imperial palace in the Ming dynasty, and survived until the early part of this century when used up in the extravagant episode of Yuan Shikai's attempted establishment of a new imperial dynasty.[86] *Zitan* is not represented in the Museum's furniture collection. Nor are the feathery-grained 'chicken-wing wood' (*jichimu*, a species of Ormosia), the dense *tieli* wood (Messua ferrea), or the native Chinese timbers such as elm and *ju* wood, the latter probably being the boldly-grained Zelkova so prevalent in the cabinetmaking of Korea and Japan.[87]

Fine furniture in the pre-Ming period seems generally to have been of lacquered wood. The fortuitously preserved eighth century cupboard in the Shōsōin temple repository in Japan (either a Chinese import or an object made to resemble Chinese imports), though now displaying the pronounced grain of Zelkova wood, was originally lacquered thickly enough to conceal it.[88] In the famous tenth century painting *The Night Banquet of Han Xizai* all the furniture shows a plain black lacquer surface,[89] evidence which can be duplicated from other early pictorial sources. The tables excavated from the late fourteenth century tomb of an imperial prince are all lacquered plain red,[90] while a text of similar date, the *Ge gu yao lun* ('Essential Criteria for Investigation of Antiquities') prescribes plain black lacquer as the finish for tables at which to play the *qin*, and assumes that the fine furniture in the home of a magnate will be of carved red lacquer or of lacquer inlaid with mother of pearl.[91]

Wang Shixiang has discovered a highly important reference from a sixteenth century source which not only suggests that plain hardwood, as opposed to lacquered, furniture was something of an innovation at that period, but points to the different statuses of the two types as markers of taste and class.[92] The author Fan Lian claims that in his youth (i.e. before about 1560) hardwood furniture was 'very rarely seen'. By the century's closing decades it was prevalent in the houses of petty bureaucrats and clerks, who used it to furnish their 'studies'. The passage is invaluable evidence for a number of reasons. Not only does it go on to point to Suzhou as a centre of hardwood furniture making, and identify craftsmen from Anhui province as being involved in its manufacture, it tells us that in the eyes of at least one member of the élite it was initially identified with a *nouveau riche* taste, the taste of a class of literate but socially despised minor functionaries. The sixteenth century in China is generally accepted to have been one of considerable social change, and the rise of this class was seen at the time as one of its most notable features. From the very beginning, doubt is cast on the modern assumption that furniture in *huali* wood represented the sole taste of the political, intellectual or social élite.

Fan Lian should not be read as meaning that hardwood furniture was unknown altogether before the sixteenth century. A couch of hardwood appears in a group portrait of three Buddhist monks dating from the fourteenth century,[93] perhaps suggesting an initially religious context for such pieces. But whatever the origins of hardwood furniture, there can be no doubt that in the late Ming lacquered furniture was at least as prominent in the homes of the ruling class and of the arbiters of taste from its ranks. This conclusion can be substantiated by pictorial and by textual evidence, most explicitly in the writings of Wen Zhenheng. On the occasions when he specifies the desirable surface for a piece of furniture his overwhelming preference is for lacquer, which he describes as best for couches, square tables, cupboards, coffers and caskets. Calligraphy tables are the only furniture type for which lacquer is taboo.[94] He has a particular penchant for the sombre tones of plain black lacquer furniture, a class of object which hardly survives at all, though occasional examples of the sort of thing Wen had in mind are known.[95] Considerable emphasis is placed upon *duanwen*, the distinctive cracking seen on old lacquer, which was the subject of a highly developed scheme of connoisseurship when applied to musical instruments.[96] This cracking must have been prevalent, for many of the objects Wen praised most lavishly were viewed as antiques in their own right, objects which were at least believed to date back hundreds of years to the Song and Yuan dynasties.

Wen Zhenheng's preference for plain lacquer is to an extent reflected in the writings of his contemporaries Gao Lian and Tu Long. It is backed up by the evidence of painting. It remained the case in the early eighteenth century, when painting tables of crackled, polished lacquer were still held superior to those of plain timber.[97] It was off lacquered furniture that the successful examination candidates of sixteenth century Peking ate.[98] And it was in lacquer beds and on lacquered couches that the sixteenth century politician Yan Song and his immediate family spent their lives.

The inventory of Yan Song's property, made in 1562, is a vital document for the study of Ming material culture, not least because it includes values for some of the pieces catalogued. Impossible to translate into modern prices, these nevertheless allow the establishment of relative values at the period. Goods which were annexed by the Imperial Household were not valued in cash. These include seventeen particularly fine beds and couches, fifteen of which are specified as being executed in a variety of lacquering techniques such as carving, inlaying and painting in gold.[99] Six hundred and forty beds were converted into cash; 355 of these are specified as being of lacquered wood and 147 of plain wood, with 138 unspecified. The list is laid out in declining value, with lacquer objects clearly being most expensive. It is headed by beds with antechambers in carved, inlaid or incised lacquer valued each at fifteen *liang* ('ounces') of silver. A single bed of *ju* (Zelkova) wood is listed at five *liang*. Down at the very end of the list come forty beds in plain lacquer or *huali* wood (one *liang* each) and, presumably for the humbler servants, 'assorted wooden beds', at a mere 0.662 *liang*.[100] This would seem to be conclusive proof that *huali* wood was not an expensive or a particularly luxurious material by the standards of the time. It is the survival into our own time of so many objects made of it, coupled with the loss of so much of the more vulnerable lacquered furniture, which has made it seem like the dominating strand in the classic furniture of the Ming and early Qing periods.

How important was furniture in the total context of the Ming and Qing interior? In the framework of a book on the subject it is easy to get this out of proportion. The anonymous author of *The Golden Lotus*, given an opportunity to describe dress or fabrics, will almost always make them the recipients of a degree of detail which implies a keen interest on the part of the reader. Furniture rarely receives this attention, with the exception of beds, which played an important symbolic role as part of the possessions a woman brought to her husband's family on marriage. The bed, together with the chests containing clothes, would be sent back to the woman's family in the event of divorce. Allowing for the necessary licence given to the author of work of fiction, it still seems that a bed could, by about 1600, be a costly item. A bed of 'decorated lacquer' is mentioned as being worth 8 *liang* of silver, while one of lacquered wood inlaid with mother of pearl is given the very high value of 60 *liang* when new, and 35 *liang* when second hand.[101] But in general the Yan Song inventory shows us how relatively inexpensive the furniture was in even the grandest of mansions. The tables, chairs and cupboards are not itemized individually, and in contrast to the beds none of them were thought worthy of confiscation in their own right. The 3,051 tables were judged worth of 0.22 *liang* each, the 2,493 chairs only 0.2 *liang* each and the 376 cupboards 0.18 *liang* each.[102] This represents 1,237.5 *liang* of Yan Song's vast wealth tied up in these necessities, a very small proportion when set for example against the 11,033.31 *liang* of golden vessels which graced these same tables.[103] When the property of one branch of the Jia family, in the eighteenth century novel *Story of the Stone*, is seized by the state, their furniture is not an important enough part of their wealth to be separately itemized.[104] Fine furniture was an important marker of status and taste, but cheap by comparison with other such markers.

Tables and Other Platforms

Early Chinese Tables

The adoption of the chair naturally brought with it the need for a raised platform at which the sitter could eat, read, write and carry out other activities. This meant the development of the high table, which like the chair is unique in the domestic life of the Chinese among the peoples of East Asia. Such a development was a process, rather than a revolution, taking place over a period of centuries from which the evidence is once again sporadic. The tenth century painting, *The Night Banquet of Han Xizai*, shows diners hunched forward on their chairs to pick at delicacies set on tables which are no higher than the seats on which they sit. However by the eleventh century the height of the table top had risen to anything from 80 to 90 cm. It was to remain largely constant between these dimensions through subsequent centuries. Tombs of the northern Song period frequently carry on their walls paintings or low relief sculptures of their owners at table, enjoying the good things of life, and these tables are of proportions familiar from later objects. A unique surviving Song dynasty table, bearing the date AD 1104, is 87.5 cm high, 69 cm wide and 84.4 cm long.[105] This object, with its plain top, circular section legs and plain, circular-section connecting bars (or 'stretchers'), brings sharply into focus one of the major problems of writing a 'history' of Chinese furniture. There is little or nothing on purely visual or constructional grounds to separate this ancient object, fortuitously preserved in the mud of a flooded town, or its numerous parallels in early painting, from a type of table, surviving in relatively large numbers, which can only be of much later date. How much later can only be a matter for speculation. The American scholar Sarah Handler has called this type of table the 'standard table', accepting that it is 'almost impossible to date'.[106] It is one of the most typical of 'types' (*shi*) in the *Classic of Lu Ban*, prevalent throughout the 'golden age' of Chinese furniture from about 1450 to 1750, and impossible to place except broadly within that band. The reasons for this phenomenon are complex. In the terms of George Kubler, whose book, *The Shape of Time*, attempts to provide a theory of how the products of the human brain and hand change through time, such a table enjoyed such a 'good entrance', in other words it so immediately and totally satisfied the needs which had brought it into being, that the process of modification common to all artefacts across the years moved so slowly as to be imperceptible.[107]

The increments by which the series of objects containing this table advanced are so small (by comparison with Chinese ceramics) that they can no longer be discerned. Hence we cannot, and perhaps may never be able to, order a number of isolated members of the series in the correct sequence. The evidence of the Chinese literature of connoisseurship seems to suggest that this is the correct interpretation. It is not that things never changed. Things made by human hand inevitably change, by a slow process of 'drift', a process made slower in the case of China by the workshop practices described in Chapter 5. But we lack the apparatus to detect the nuances of change, the weak 'signals' which individual objects of Chinese furniture emit.

Rectangular Tables

This does not mean that we cannot order the surviving material evidence at all. One of the most useful tools for doing so has been provided by Wang Shixiang, with his division of the Chinese tables surviving today into the two categories of *an*, 'tables with set-in legs' and *zhuo* 'tables with legs at the corners'.[108] Thus 46 and 47 are both square dining tables, but 46 is an example of the *an* while 47 is an example of the *zhuo*. This distinction is a most useful one, and will be adhered to in characterizing the material here. However it is not clear how far back this division of terminology holds good. Imprecision and looseness are more characteristic of Ming and Qing sources. Thus a table of the present type appears in a Ming illustrated child's primer under yet another word for table, *tai*.[109] Differences of regional dialect compound the confusion. The *Classic of Lu Ban* has this form under the heading *yi zi zhuo shi* 'character one table type'. The Chinese word for 'one' is written as a single horizontal stroke, and hence the name refers to any long thin table. The text, despite using the word *zhuo* (which it will be remembered in modern Chinese usage ought to mean table with legs at the corners) clearly states that the top protrudes over the legs at the ends. Though the

28 dimensions in the text would give a table considerably shorter than the Museum's example, the accompanying woodblock illustration shows one almost identical in style and proportions.[110]

Whether it is more correctly designated a *pingtou an* (Wang Shixiang), *yi zi zhuo* (*Classic of Lu Ban*) or a 'standard table' (Handler), there is no doubt that this, and its only slightly less plain counterpart, were ubiquitous in Ming and Qing households at all social levels. Such tables had numerous uses. Any attempt to classify Chinese furniture strictly by function will fail on the grounds that many pieces were used in a number of ways, according to different needs and contexts.

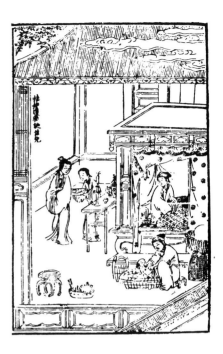

29 *Woodblock illustration* from the collection *Chan zhen yi shi* 'Anecdotes of Zen and Tao', Tianqi period (1621–1627).

Following page Above:

28 *Table, huali* wood. About 1550–1750, height 74.5 cm, length of top 180 cm, width of top 54 cm, FE.119–1978.

Below:

30 *Table, huali* wood. About 1550–1650, height 32 cm, length of top 195.5 cm, width of top 55.7 cm, W.7–1969.

Thus very plain, rectangular tables with in-set legs can be seen in Ming woodblock illustration in use for casual meals, as a writing desk and as a table set against walls for the display of flowers and ornamental pieces.[111] They are very commonly seen in bedroom scenes in Ming dynasty illustrated books. As noted above, the large canopied bed provided a platform on which much of the informal activity of daily life took place. A long rectangular table stood at the side of the bed, ready to be moved in front of it at any time. Tables of both the *zhuo* and *an* types were used in this way as dressing tables for both men and women, writing and painting surfaces or simply as something to lean on when lying on the bed.[112] Both men and women of the upper classes used them for casual meals in their rooms when no guests were present.[113] The tomb of Wang Xijue, who died in 1611, contains wooden models of furniture mainly for use in the bedroom (though a *guan mao yi* armchair is included as well); canopied bed, clothes rack and a long table with in-set legs for dining.[114]

The basic constructional unit of the Chinese table remains the mitred frame with a central floating panel, which may be formed of one or more planks. With the exception of some solid-topped tables, where a single massive piece of wood takes the place of such a construction, this unit is common to all tables of the Ming and Qing periods whether in plain or lacquered wood. It is seen on both the Museum's examples of the 'character "one" table', though they differ in other respects. The simpler of the two (which has been cut down in the legs by 6.5 cm in modern times)[115] has circular section legs and stretchers. Below the top is a plain strip (or 'apron'), held in place only by the legs. A slot is cut in the leg for the piece of wood (a 'spandrel') which curves down from the apron to appear on either side of the top of each leg. The leg, fixed by tenons into the underside of the top, holds the spandrel in place, while the joints between the spandrel and the apron hold the apron in place.

The same basic construction is seen on a table with rounded rectangular section legs. Here the apron has a raised (or 'beaded') edge running continuously round the edge of the spandrel. The spandrel in turn is carved into a shape seen in many areas of Chinese applied art from the thirteenth century onwards, a *yuntou* 'cloud head' or *ruyi tou* 'as-you-wish head'.[116] One difference in the construction of the two tables is that on the first the joint between the spandrel and apron is at 45° (i.e. it is 'mitred') while on the second the same joint is along a line parallel to the table top.

If these two can serve to represent the classic *an* type of table, the classic *zhuo* type with the legs set at the corners is represented by a small table, the simplicity and standard proportions of which make a precise dating equally impossible. In terms of the *Classic of Lu Ban* this

31 *Detail of* FE.119–1978.

32 *Detail of* W.7–1969.

is a *xiao qin zhuo shi*, 'small *qin* table type'.[117] The *qin*, a rectangular stringed musical instrument plucked with the right hand and stopped with the left, was indeed played at just such a type of table, as graphic sources confirm.[118] However the name should not make us think that this was the sole use for such tables. One has only to think of the western 'coffee table', with its varied functions other than the consumption of coffee, to see that there is no necessary total identification between name and function. In fact, such tables were as likely to be used in the context of formal dining.

The Ming or Qing dinner party did not assume any single invariable form. However one thing about the most formal parties which struck a sixteenth century Dutch writer as odd was that one small table was provided for each diner, rather than the great feasting boards familiar to him from Europe:

> 'The manner of their banquetings and feastes are thus, as many persons as are invited, so many tables are prepared and made ready, although they be a hundreth: the tables are very faire and finely painted, with all kinds of imagerie and flowers most pleasant to behold, so that they use no table cloths, but round about the edges of the table there hangeth a cloth down to the ground, of silke, damaske, gold or silver, every according to his estate...'[119]

The author, van Linschoten, is here clearly talking about lacquered furniture, but his remarks apply equally to hardwood tables such as this one. The textile table frontals (in seventeenth century usage *zhuo wei*)[120] he reported were an equally important part of the interior, and it is worth pointing out that their wide use suggests an aesthetic considerably less interested in revealing the structure of the object than that which the modern viewer, perhaps conditioned by a functionalist perspective, might find appropriate.

There is more to the distinction between *an* and *zhuo* types of table than the disposition of the legs at the corners. The *zhuo* is of itself slightly less stable, and hence the legs are often connected on all four sides by stretchers, which counteract the tendency of the legs to splay when downward pressure is applied to the top. The *zhuo* also often displays, as Wang Shixiang was the first to point out, the combination of a recessed 'waist' beneath the top with the bulging feet known as *mati* 'horsehoofs'. Wang convincingly derives the recessed waist, or *shuyao*, from architectural features, chiefly the stone pediments of buildings. The term itself is mentioned in early architectural treatises.[121] The almost invariable combination of the recessed waist with horsehoof feet is seen by Wang as one of the 'grammatical rules' of classic Chinese furniture construction. In his terminology, and that

34 *Woodblock illustration* from the drama *Fen xiang ji* 'A Record of Burning Incense', late Ming edition.

33 *Table*, *huali* wood. About 1550–1650, height 87.7 cm, length of top 99 cm, width of top 48.8 cm, FE.21–1980.

Above:

35 *Low table*, *huali* wood. About 1550–1650, but cut down in the twentieth century, height 45 cm, length of top 94 cm, width of top 61 cm, FE.20–1980.

Below:

36 *Low table*, *huali* wood. About 1550–1600, but cut down in the twentieth century, height of 50.2 cm, length of top 97.5 cm, width of top 48 cm, FE.112–1981.

used by twentieth century cabinetmakers working in continuation of late Qing tradition, such a table is a *jiezhuo* 'prolonging table' i.e. one used to lengthen an existing dining table. Single dining tables of the *an* form are *jiu* 'wine' *an*.[122] The legs of such tables are worked from a single piece of timber, resulting in a loss of wood for most of the length above the horsehoof's bulge. The Museum collection contains two examples of what were originally *qin* tables where the legs have been cut down from around the usual 85 cm to 45 and 50 cm respectively. This was almost certainly done in Peking in the early twentieth century, to satisfy a demand on the part of western customers for low furniture which could not be met by genuine surviving examples. Tables proportioned in this way almost always turn out to have been cut down, the horsehoof being formed by grafting on two shaped blocks cut from the discarded lower portion of the leg. The detail of the bottom of the horsehoof reveals the join. Very occasionally the legs on a low table will appear on examination to be solid, but in such cases the legs may have been shortened by the much more elaborate expedient of detaching the legs from the top, cutting off an upper portion, recutting the joints and refitting the legs. Evidence of this process will be found by examining the inside of the leg where it meets the top, and where extra blocks will have been added to make the thickness of what was once the middle of the leg up to that necessary to stabilize the joint.

A small table which may also have been a *jiu an* 'wine table'[123] has close similarities with a long rectangular type of table such as 30. It is rendered slightly unusual however by the solid flanges set into the short ends of the top, which are much more generally associated with tables intended not for eating but for display. Indeed it is not impossible that the piece has been the subject of considerable alteration, as the spandrels of the legs are also of unusual construction, being formed of two pieces which are not mitred but are joined along a line parallel to the top.

The large versions of the design with a raised flange at the ends of the top are called *qiaotou an* 'raised end tables' by modern Chinese writers, while the type appears occasionally in western sources as an 'altar table'. There is evidence that such tables were employed in the domestic cult of ancestors, supporting flower vases, burners for incense and offerings of food and drink, but they were equally common in secular contexts, set against walls as surfaces on which to show antiques or contemporary art objects, flowers and the paraphernalia for enjoying incense simply as an elegant relaxation.[124] They do not appear in the *Classic of Lu Ban*, but the evidence from Ming and Qing sources is that they were sometimes called *bi zhuo*, 'wall tables'. Wen Zhenheng tells us that such tables, which may have raised corners, should not be too

37 *Detail* of FE.20–1980, showing detail of altered food.

41 *Woodblock illustration* from the novel *Jin ping mei* 'The Golden Lotus', chapter 7, 1616 edition.

38 *Table*, *huali* wood. About 1550–1650, height 85 cm, length of top 99 cm, width of top 46 cm, FE.121–1978.

39 *Detail* of FE.121–1978, showing spandrel.

40 *Table, huali* wood. About 1600, height 89 cm, length of top 177 cm, width of top 41.3 cm, FE.18–1980.

42 *Detail* of FE.18–1980, showing openwork carved panel between legs.

wide.[125] A table of this type could sometimes have a solid top, in which case it was a *tianran ji* 'natural' (in the sense of unworked) table. Wen Zhenheng is very precise about these:

> 'Natural tables are made of wood with a pattern in the grain, such as *huali*, *tieli* or *xiangnan*. Only the large ones are valuable, though the length should not exceed 8 feet and the thickness 5 inches. The end flanges must not be too sharp, but smooth and rounded which is the antique pattern. Those which have footstretchers below like Japanese tables are even more curious. They should not have four legs like a writing table, nor be set into old tree roots. Rather use a piece of thick, wide timber for the top, hollow it out and lightly carve it with designs as clouds and *ruyi*. Do not carve the vulgar patterns such as dragons, phoenixes, flowers and grasses. The long narrow ones made in recent times are abominable.'[126]

Abominable or not, a *tianran ji* could be a huge piece of furniture. The writer Zhang Dai recorded seeing one of *tieli* wood in 1663 which from his account must have been about a metre wide and over five metres long, and which had cost its owner two hundred gold pieces.[127] A surviving example dated 1640–41 is 343 cm in length.[128]

42   The Museum's example, its end panels carved in openwork with a design of dragons and floral scrolls, might have seemed 'vulgar' to Wen Zhenheng. However by the early eighteenth century it would have been a valued Ming antique, just the sort of thing to attract Zhou Erxue, writing in the early 1730s. For him, the important point is that a wall table should be supported on solid panels rather than individual legs:

> 'For wall tables choose plain *zitan* or *tiemu* of a refined and antique style. Polish them often and in time they will become glossy and shine like a mirror. The vulgar style with thick legs have the nickname "Doug Qichang (1555–1636, the famous painter and arbiter of taste) tables". I have often proclaimed this an injustice to him. They should be discarded and never used.'[129]

Despite these strictures, display tables of the Qing period seem generally to have had four legs, as those with solid panels came to be
43 seen as antique curiosities. A fine eighteenth century example shows all the precision of finish and eclecticism of decorative content which
44 characterizes the highest quality crafts of the period. On this piece the timber of the top panel contrasts with the lighter wood of the top frame and the legs. This seems to have been a feature distinctive to the period, and such a use of contrasting woods is often seen in the

44 *Detail* of FE.76–1983, showing carving of apron.

records of tables manufactured in the palace workshops in the Yongzheng period (1723–1735).[130] The raised roundels on the apron are a motif whose origins lie in metalwork and jade carving of the pre-imperial period some two thousand years earlier, which enjoyed renewed popularity from the Qianlong period (1736–1795) with the publication of several illustrated catalogues of such designs. The continuing use made of these designs at a later date can be seen on a
45 nineteenth century table, the elaborate apron of which is partly structural and partly decorative, with its openwork carving of stylized dragons and the jade ritual disks known as *bi.*

Square Tables

As discussed above, formal feasts often involved one small table per guest. However we have also seen that long rectangular tables were used for less formal meals. In fact written and visual evidence shows that almost any combination of types of table with any number of diners existed at some stage, according to convenience and the degree of lavishness of the entertainment. One common type of dining table was the *ba xian zhuo*, 'Eight Immortals table', a square table seating two on each side, hence its name. The *ba xian zhuo* in the *Classic of Lu Ban* is a small rectangular table,[131] though Wang Shixiang posits a corruption in the text here, since all other evidence shows them to have been square. Wen Zhenheng did not approve of them:

> 'In square tables the old lacquered ones are the finest. You must
> favour those which are extremely square, large, antique and
> plain, seating a dozen or so people at once for the enjoyment
> and display of calligraphy and painting. Recently made tables of
> "Eight Immortals" and such patterns are useful only for feasting
> and are not objects of elegance.'[132]

A square table, in black lacquer with a marble top, can indeed be seen being used for the connoisseurship of art in a painting dated 1437.[133] Such a piece might well have survived into Wen's day, though none is known today. His complaint makes it clear that the 'vulgar' square dining table was in widespread use. The difficulty in interpreting the scattered Ming evidence for the place of furniture in culture and society is illustrated by an entry in the work of Wen Zhenheng's close contemporary, Gu Qiyuan (1565–1628). Writing of his native Nanjing, he argues that the square *ba xian zhuo* was a manifestation of the plain, old-fashioned and unpretentious customs of the fifteenth century, while by the Jiajing period (1522–1566) it was general practice in upper class circles to seat two guests to a table.[134]

46 *Square table*, *huali* wood. About 1550–1600, height 85.7 cm, top 95 x 94.5 cm, FE.67–1983, Addis Bequest.

Once again the complex social stratification, regional variation and personal taste differentiation of Ming China subverts any attempt to produce simple formulae.

46,47   The Museum's two square tables of themselves are enough to confirm this complexity in the area of style. Though probably fairly close in date, they are designed on the basis of very different aesthetic considerations. The *an* with its inset legs is characterized by a lack of decoration, while the *zhuo*, originally one of a pair, shows elaborate freehand carving of the dragon brackets, low relief scrolling, and a complex curving edge to the apron. One could speculate that, as in most pre-machine craft cultures, work was an index of value, rendering the elaborately carved piece more valuable, more expensive. Such elaboration only makes sense by contrast with contemporary, simpler workmanship. Neither table is in fact exactly square, and the very slight variation in the length of the sides can probably be explained by the periodic practice of dismantling the top frame and shaving down the mitre on one side to tighten up the joint.

Opposite

43 *Table*, *huali* and *hongmu* woods. About 1740–1780, height 84 cm length of top 140.5 cm, width of top 37.6 cm, FE.76–1983, Addis Bequest.

45 *Table*, *hongmu* wood. About 1800–1850, height 80 cm, length of top 126.5 cm, width of top 39.5 cm, FE.4–1971.

48 *Detail* of FE.19–1980.

The joints fixing the legs of the square *zhuo* to the frame of the top throw further interesting light on working practices in Ming cabinetmaking. To put it at its simplest, different joints are employed on two of the legs of the same piece. On one of them, the bulging upper section of the leg, which fits over the circular section main leg, is carved from a single piece of wood. On one of the other legs, this block is in three pieces, with two side pins between the 'bulge' and the main leg. The photograph shows the 'bulge' and one of these pins, which has split in two, a part of it remaining glued to the main housing. Rather than being evidence of a repair or reconstruction, this three-piece leg mounting may represent a simpler way of doing it, one employed by the carpenter on discovering how difficult it was to carve the one-piece mounting.[135] Such flexibility is the other side of the coin from the rigorous adherence to pattern and precedent implied in the more standardized construction of the square *an*. It is also incidentally valuable in demonstrating that Chinese carpenters were not afraid to use adhesives when the situation demanded it. The western conception that glue and nails were taboo in the manufacture of Chinese furniture is very long-lived. Perhaps one of the earliest pieces of Chinese domestic hardwood furniture to reach the West was the canopied bed in *huali* wood acquired by the Elector of Brandenburg–Prussia in 1710. To his anonymous cataloguer, 'The curiosity of this bed frame lies in the fact that there is no nail in it.'[136] The idea that the eschewal of glue and nails (not in any case the invariable practice of real Chinese carpenters) denotes not only ingeniousness of workmanship but moral superiority tells us more about western images of China than it does about Chinese workshop practice.

49 *Detail* of FE.19–1980, showing knee block of leg with separate pin.

47 *Square table*, *huali* wood. About 1550–1600, height 84.5 cm, top 96.2 x 95.8 cm, FE.19–1980.

Kang Tables

One significant group of tables, of strikingly different proportions to those already discussed, is well represented in the collection, as in most western collections. The fortuitous resemblance of these low tables to the coffee table made them eagerly sought by early collectors. These are the so-called 'kang tables'. A kang is a hollow brick platform, built into a room and heated by a fire underneath it, which served in the harsh winter of north China as a bed and general living space. Widespread at all levels of society until the early part of this century, the brick kang provided an intimate and informal context in which some of the body-language of ancient China, its squatting and kneeling postures, was preserved. As well as cushions for the back and arms, the kang in a wealthy household would be provided with small tables for tea, spittoons, snacks and other conveniences. Yet to call all such small low tables 'kang tables' is slightly misleading. They are just as likely to have been employed on a ta, the freestanding couch of wood which was in the southern parts of China the main venue for this sphere of daily life. The type is not mentioned either in the *Classic of Lu Ban* or in the connoisseurship literature, a reflection of its familiar domestic status.

Just like the kang and couches on which they stood, such small tables (to which the name kang table now adheres so firmly that it would be pedantic to alter it) vary greatly in size. A lacquered example inlaid in mother of pearl is close to the minimum, affording room only for a single tea-cup. Larger hardwood examples show the variations within the form, though a majority of kang tables are zhuo, with recessed waist and legs set at the corners. Most of them have the double-curving legs called Chinese tanglang tui 'praying mantis legs', or xiangbi tui 'elephant trunk legs'. However variations in the construction even of this fairly basic type can be seen by comparing the undersides of two tables which it would be impossible to separate by date on purely aesthetic grounds. Both clearly show the transverse braces, common to all the types of table above (except, obviously, those with tops worked from a single plank). On one table the tenons of the outer two braces are visible on the outside edge of the top frame. On the other none of the braces have exposed tenons. On the first, the apron on the long sides is secured by a single large peg, set slightly off-centre to avoid the tenon of the central brace. On the second table, which lacks the device of through-tenoning (identified generally by Ellsworth as an 'early' feature) these pegs are more freely employed, with two on each long side and one on each short. Pegs too have been claimed as an 'early' feature of joinery,[137] leaving us with contradictory evidence from these two technical features. It

50 *Kang table*, *huali* wood. About 1550–1600, height 25 cm, length of top 70.5 cm, width of top 49 cm, FE.68–1983, Addis Bequest.

51 *Miniature table or stand*, black lacquer inlaid with mother of pearl on a wood core. About 1660–1720, height 14.1 cm, top 30 x 30 cm, FE.25–1985.

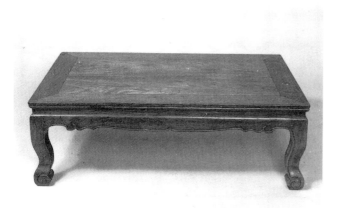

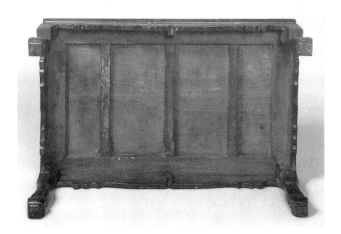

52 *Kang table*, *huali* wood. About 1550–1600, height 29.5 cm, length of top 91.5 cm, width of top 57 cm, FE.120–1978.

54 *Underside* of FE.120–1978, showing pins on apron.

53 *Kang table*, *huali* wood. About 1550–1650, height 31.5 cm, length of top 100.5 cm, width of top 65.3 cm, W.8–1969.

55 *Underside* of W.7–1969.

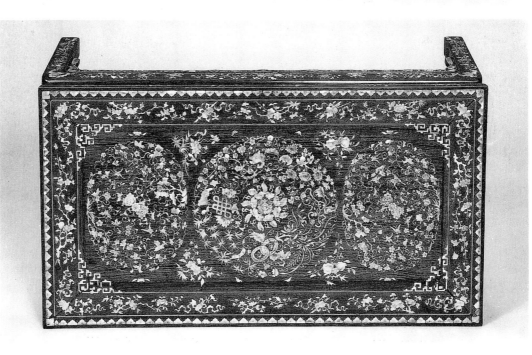

56 *Kang table*, wood inlaid with mother of pearl. About 1865, height 26 cm, length of top 78 cm, width of top 42.3 cm, 652–'69.

57 *Top* of 652–'69.

remains very difficult to order the tables in a totally satisfactory chronological sequence on the basis of developments in technique. Another distinction between the two tables is that the second has a beaded raised edge to the top, called a *lan shui xian* and supposedly used on tables associated with eating and drinking to act as a barrier to any spilled liquids. The first, and possibly on stylistic grounds the earlier, table is without this handy feature.

56 The Museum's earliest Chinese furniture acquisition is a *kang* table. Described at the time as being of walnut wood, the table was bought at the Paris International Exhibition of 1867 for £24. The fine and
57 elaborate inlay of mother-of-pearl has close affinities with contemporary textile design, particularly with the embroidered roundels used to decorate women's garments. It is also visibly related to inlay work produced in Hanoi in the late nineteenth and early twentieth centuries by immigrant craftsman from Canton, where this piece was probably made.[138]

When taken in formal circumstances, seated in a reception hall, tea demanded high stands for the cups and other paraphernalia. These stands, *cha ji*, were often made as sets with matching chairs. An
58 elaborately decorated example in painted lacquer is typical of the eighteenth century not only in its eclectic use of ornament from a variety of sources, but in the greatly enlarged role given to the recessed waist, the *shuyao* between the top and the beginning of the legs. This enlargement of the waist is a feature generally observable on many pieces of furniture of mid- and late-Qing date.

58 *Stand*, polychrome painted lacquer on a wood core. About 1730–1800, height 67 cm, top 40.3 x 40.3 cm, W.82–1923.

The Chinese Furniture Industry

The Centres of Manufacture

Where was fine furniture made in the Ming and Qing periods? The great majority of the population obviously had to make do with the products of local village or small town carpenters, working in locally available woods with perhaps no more than a simple coating of plain lacquer. However by the sixteenth century at the very latest China had developed a unified domestic market in luxury craft products. This meant that the moneyed élite in all parts of the empire could expect to obtain fine teas from Fujian, brocaded silk textiles from Nanjing, writing paper, ink and brushes from northern Anhui, and ceramics from Yixing and Jingdezhen. There is no unequivocal evidence for the primacy of one city or area in the furniture trade, though evidence does suggest that, in the sixteenth and seventeenth centuries, the centre of production of the most covetable pieces was in the lower Yangtze valley, the most populous and the wealthiest part of China at that time.

The conventional wisdom among western connoisseurs in the twentieth century has been that the city of Suzhou, not far inland from modern Shanghai, 'was a furniture making center where the finest cabinet work was done.'[139] However evidence that hardwood furniture was actually manufactured there at any time before this century is very sparse. The 1539 *Gazetteer* of Suzhou mentions only bamboo furniture as being made there, and as being a particular speciality.[140] This information appears in subsequent editions of the *Gazetteer* up to the end of the nineteenth century, and is confirmed by other sources. In 1671, Li Yu wrote, *a propos* of chairs, stools and benches:

> 'On the basis of period, new is better than old. On the basis
> of place, northern is not as good as southern. The wooden
> pieces of Yangzhou and the bamboo pieces of Suzhou can
> be said to be the best of all time, and hold the first place
> throughout the empire.'[141]

Yangzhou had indeed been known as a centre of luxury furniture-making at least from the Tang dynasty.[142] The author of a detailed account of Suzhou's cultural and commercial attractions in the early nineteenth century makes no mention of hardwood furniture as a speciality, but refers again to the 'light and delightful' stands, couches, tables, chairs, cupboards, stools, prams and hammocks of 'purple bamboo'.[143] There is no doubt however that there *was* a major furniture industry in Suzhou in pre-modern times. We have already noted a reference to its existence in the writing of Fan Lian. In 1620 Wen Zhenheng, himself a resident of Suzhou, could refer casually to a specific type of chair, 'the meditation chair from Zhuanzhu lane', if only to condemn it as a vulgar type inadmissible to the homes of the stylish.[144] ('Zhuanzhu lane' was one of Suzhou's chief centres of craftworking, noted in particular for its jade carving ateliers. Wen may have been referring to chairs carved from seemingly naturally sinuous wood). What is in doubt is that Suzhou enjoyed unchallenged prestige in pre-modern times as *the* centre of fine cabinet making. By the mid-nineteenth century it was believed by foreigners that:

> '...any thing superb,...must be sent for from Soo-chow – fine
> pictures, fine carved work, fine silks and fine ladies, all come
> from Soo-chow.'[145]

It seems in fact more likely that the craft was diffused through a number of the more prosperous cities of south-central China, able to tap a market in the imported hardwood timbers, able to deploy craftsmen skilled in cabinet making and in lacquering, and able to serve a concentration of wealthy clients. Back in the 1620s Wen Zhenheng was already implying that specific types of furniture came from areas other than Suzhou city itself. It came from the neighbouring counties of Wujiang (bamboo chairs) and Yongjia (folding beds), from Canton (folding beds) and from Peking (lacquered furniture). Small pieces were also imported for the elegant interior from Japan.[146] This would explain Li Yu's statement about Yangzhou as the source of the finest wooden chairs. It would explain several references in the sixteenth century novel *The Golden Lotus* to 'Nanjing beds' as the finest available and the statement in the same book by a smooth-tongued matchmaker that, 'Such a good family would be impossible to find – all their furniture comes from Nanjing.'[147] It would explain too the presentations of (presumably locally manufactured) furniture from a high official based in Nanjing to the emperor in Peking in the 1670s. These gifts included a sedan chair, a table of *tieli* wood and a folding screen, almost certainly a lacquered screen, decorated with a design of antiques.[148]

In addition to procurement from the south, the Ming imperial court in Peking was able to have pieces of furniture made in workshops under its immediate control. The description of the administrative functions of the *Yu yong jian*, a eunuch-staffed office, includes:

> 'They manufacture all items of wood, such as screens and couches,
> and all bibelots of *zitan* wood, ivory, ebony and lacquer inlaid
> with mother-of-pearl for use in the Imperial Presence.'[149]

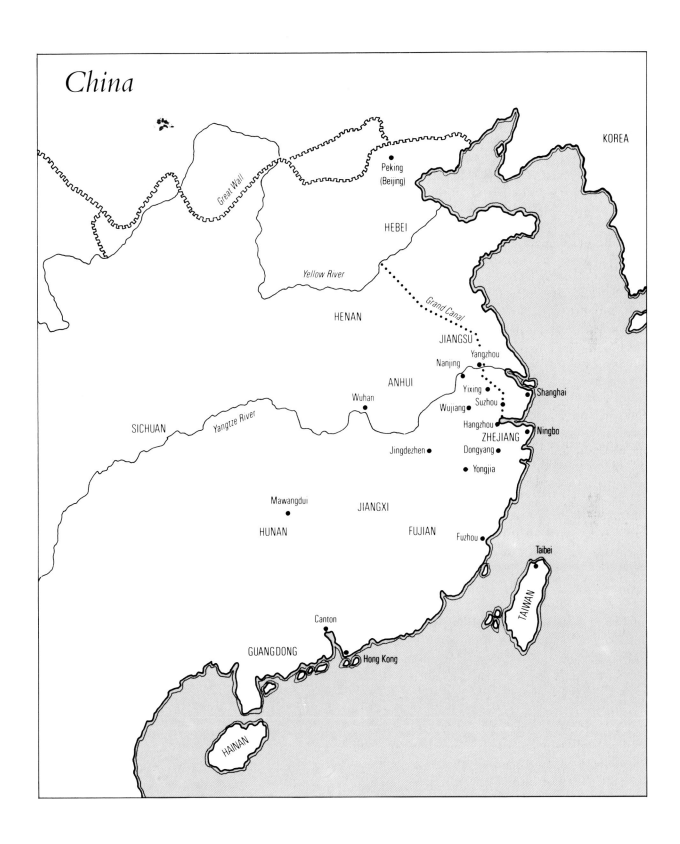

China

KOREA

Great Wall

Peking
(Beijing)

HEBEI

Yellow River

Grand Canal

HENAN

JIANGSU

Yangzhou

Nanjing

ANHUI

Yixing

Shanghai

Wuhan

Wujiang

Suzhou

SICHUAN

Yangtze River

Hangzhou

Ningbo

ZHEJIANG

Jingdezhen

Dongyang

Yongjia

Mawangdui

JIANGXI

HUNAN

FUJIAN

Fuzhou

Taibei

TAIWAN

Canton

GUANGDONG

Hong Kong

HAINAN

The cabinet workshop of this bureau was described in the early seventeenth century as employing 'several hundred men'.[150]

In the succeeding Qing period, this function of supplying items for the court came under the Imperial Household Department, which maintained workshops in a number of crafts in Peking and elsewhere, permanently employing some kinds of craftsman and hiring others for shorter terms to fulfill specific projects. Into this latter category fall the few furniture makers whose names, fortuitously preserved in the palace archives until this century, have come down to us. Although these records, which have been studied for the years 1723–1736 by the Chinese scholar Zhu Jiajin, do not allow us to estimate the total size of the palace furniture workshop, they do give us the names of some of its staff, categorized as: wood workers, rush matting workers (who made woven seats), oil workers, coloured lacquer workers, lacquer workers, inlay workers, bronze workers and carvers. In all cases where a place of origin is mentioned for these men, it is invariably either Suzhou or Canton, the latter city being one to which a body of evidence points as being another important source of luxury furniture.[151] Li Yu singles out chests in *huali* and *zitan* woods as being a speciality of the city.[152] A Portuguese visitor in the sixteenth century remarked on the splendour of the wooden beds inlaid with ivory made there, and on the massive pairs of cupboards which adorned formal reception rooms, as well as on lacquered wooden furniture, an exotic commodity to the first western traders to visit China.[153] There must have been a continuous tradition of furniture making in Canton which spanned the second half of the seventeenth century when European ships rarely came here. From 1720 onwards there is a huge amount of evidence surviving in Europe that Cantonese workshops could supply not only lacquered pieces, mostly in the painted gold on black style which was the regional speciality, but also pieces in *huali* and other hardwoods. These exhibit many of the technical features and all of the technical skill of the best work in the domestic design tradition. It seems unlikely that Canton could manufacture objects after western patterns in these woods, while remaining detached from the internal market in furniture. Certainly in early twentieth century Peking the city of Canton was proverbial among furniture dealers as being the source of the finest workmanship, *Guang zuo*, 'Canton work' as opposed to the less desirable *Jing zuo* 'Peking work'.[154] Some lacquered pieces of furniture can be assigned to Canton on the basis of their technical features, but the wide geographical distribution of woodworking and lacquering across China as a whole make it, and will always make it, impossible to assign the bulk of surviving pieces to specific workshops or regions.

The Organization of Workshops

Evidence on the organization of units of production within the traditional furniture industry is sparse in the extreme. Like many other craftsmen, carpenters were organized in guilds, locally rather than nationally based, which existed to promote group solidarity through worship of a common founding father of the craft (such as Lu Ban), to enforce conditions of apprenticeship and standards of work, and to engage in concerted action for the establishment of conditions of work and rates of pay. Suzhou saw its first craft guilds established in the late sixteenth century, but the carpenters do not appear to have been among the first groups to so organize. The *Xiao mu gongsuo*, 'Guild of Fine Woodwork', was set up there only in 1810, and refounded in 1844. A *Qiao mu gongsuo*, 'Guild of Fancy Woodwork', was set up in 1821.[155] These relatively late dates are supported by the evidence from Peking, where the *Lu Ban sheng hui*, 'Sacred Society of Lu Ban', though claiming an origin lost in the mists of antiquity, actually seems to have been formed around 1850.[156] This guild included both architectural woodworkers and cabinetmakers, the latter still being active enough in the guild to offer information and assistance to the German scholar Gustav Ecke in the 1920s.

It seems probable that in the Ming and earlier Qing periods the makers of furniture acted as their own retailers, and that specialist furniture shops did not exist. However by about 1870 Peking saw the establishment for the first time of a *Zhuo yi hang*, 'Guild of Tables and Chairs', an association of shopkeepers, whose apprentices studied not cabinetmaking but book-keeping.[157]

Family tradition as well as regional factors played a strong part in determining entry to the furniture-making craft. In those Chinese crafts, such as lacquering, bamboo carving and woodblock printing, where enough information survives to allow sketchy biographies of individuals to be built up, the direction of a workshop almost always remains within the same surname for a number of generations. The habit of taking apprentices from within one's own family group or at least from one's own native area meant that as late as 1965 90% of the decorative woodcarvers working in Shanghai were originally from nearby Dongyang county, where the craft had been a local speciality at least since the late nineteenth century. The traditional apprenticeship, seen in Hong Kong almost to the present day, lasted three years and three months. The first year was often spent in totally menial tasks, and even at the end of it the journeyman was as likely as not unable to operate as a totally independent maker, since the practice of concealing the more subtle 'tricks of the trade' was widespread.[158]

Apart from the individual itinerant carpenter, who visited even the most remote villages, most woodworkers in the luxury end of the craft worked in groups, under the leadership of the workshop owner. The illustrations to the early editions of the *Classic of Lu Ban* never show more than two or three men working together, and never show two men working simultaneously on the same piece of furniture. The practice of one worker carrying out all the stages to produce a piece of furniture from start to finish remains current in the fine reproduction furniture industry in Hong Kong at the present time. Some furniture workshops of a very traditional type studied on Taiwan in this century all employed less than ten workers. It took nineteen of them to cater to the needs of the 28,000 residents of the town of Lugang as well as trade throughout the island.[159] The seventeenth century novel *A Marriage to Astonish the Age* reveals that a specialist coffin making workshop could contain as many as eight men, able to produce a fully finished coffin for a very wealthy woman in half-a-day.[160]

This impressive speed of working raises the possibility of the prefabrication of furniture parts. This was certainly done in the workshops of eighteenth century New England, where considerable stocks of parts of the most common components (legs, splats, back rails, etc.) were maintained. Given the very common nature of a chair such as 6 or a table such as 28, the possibly of such stockpiling cannot be overlooked. It has been pointed out, with regard to the early Philadelphian furniture industry, that:

> 'Within each shop all of the workers understood what plain feet were to look like and how much work plain splats required. In a very competitive traditional industry, where the possibilities of technical advances were strictly limited, any radical departure could give a market edge, and would be immediately imitated.'

This recipe for stylistic homogeneity, and possibly for rather slow stylistic change, seems applicable to the situation in China, as does the suggestion (again referring to the American evidence) that, 'The final object was rarely the product of a single design', but rather a combination of existing designs in a new way.[161]

The Designing of Furniture

The nature of design in pre-modern China has received little attention. It seems natural within the western tradition, and indeed it is built into the etymology of the word, that a 'design' for an object should in some way be a graphic, two-dimensional representation of a three-dimensional thing, or in other words a picture. The modern Chinese word for 'design', *tu'an* certainly reflects this. However the *Classic of Lu Ban*, almost our sole source for the maker's point of view, treats of 35 *shi*, 'types', using a word which has no necessary connotations of a picture. Indeed a *shi* can be, and in this text is, embodied in a string of words as a purely verbal description. 'Types' had names, and these verbal snapshots were enough to identify an object within the slow changing classic style of the period c.1550 to c.1750. Thus a table such as 46 could be encapsulated in the formula, *yi tui san ya luoguo cheng fang zhuo*, 'square table with three aprons at each leg and hunchback stretchers'. This would always mean the same kind of table.[162] These formulae were transmitted orally, rather than written down, often in the form of *ge jue*, mnemonic rhymes which played an important part in the learning of a craft in a culture where rote learning was the major form of instruction.[163] The series of poems on various crafts by the seventeenth century writer Pu Songling are an annexation by the lettered classes of this form of pre-literate, popular culture. Some carpenters would have possessed at least minimal literacy, as the practice has been recorded of using characters taken from the child's reading primer *The Thousand Character Classic* as a sort of 'ABC' to mark furniture parts prior to assembly.[164] These marks, and others like them, are frequently seen on eighteenth century furniture for the western export market. It is also the case that drawn preparatory designs were used in the palace workshops, where they were often executed by specialist designers. The administrative head of the workshops in the 1720s, a Manchu named Haiwang, was himself one of these designers.[165] But in general the use of preparatory paper work was less important than the workmanship of habit developed since childhood. The carpenters shown in *The Classic of Lu Ban* were in the same state as their English contemporaries, described by Samuel Pepys as having, 'their knowledge lying in their hands confusedly.'[166]

The descriptive power of the 'type' can only have been strengthened by the seeming prevalence of close personal contact between customer and maker. Many kinds of workers in the luxury crafts, such as silver-smiths, tailors and window-lattice makers, are known to have visited the homes of customers, bringing tools and raw materials, and to have worked there under immediate supervision. Several *Classic of Lu Ban* illustrations show carpenters working under the eye of a figure in the long gown of the minority of Chinese who never engaged in manual labour. These may be workshop owners, but equally they may be customers. Li Yu, writing in 1671, is illuminating on the immediacy of this contact. From his eulogy of the drawer as one of the ultimate conveniences of life, something which 'handles your idleness and conceals your incompetence', it is evident that he expected to have drawers installed in all new furniture simply by specifying their addition to the craftsman at the time of manufacture. He is even more categorical on the subject of wedges, for fixing tables on uneven stone or rammed earth flowers. He says of them:

> 'These do not have to be bought with money, but only
> involve the customer in the effort of opening his mouth as
> the craftsman is about to wield his axe, and the servants in
> the effort of lifting their hands. Then one can have a limitless
> supply which will be of endless use.'[167]

Li Yu's numerous other inventions, such as heated chairs, cooled stools and various sophisticated forms of bed shelf and curtain, are all predicated on being able to explain these quirky and presumably novel requirements directly to the carpenter.

The Status of Cabinetmaking

Given this close contact, the generally low esteem felt by the élite for the craft of cabinetmaking is puzzling. The products of the craft were extremely important to the ordering of the elegant setting for élite life, as the detail of Wen Zhenheng's prescriptions and proscriptions shows. However the studied lack of interest in the makers of furniture, by contrast with the degree of intimate patronage of bamboo carvers and workers in bronze and jade in the Ming and Qing periods, is reflected in the failure to record the names of craftsman, outside the official documents of the palace workshops. This is analogous to the attitude taken in contemporary sources to the craftspeople involved in the manufacture of fashionable dress – stylish clothing was of great importance to the rich but we do not know the name of a single Ming or Qing tailor. That it was carpentry which engaged the interest of the last-but-one feckless emperor of the Ming dynasty is recorded with unspoken contempt.[168] For the Son of Heaven to engage in manual work as an amusement was decadent enough, but for him to engage in woodworking was inexplicable.

We do not know what the emperor's toolkit may have looked like, but it is certainly the case that Chinese woodworking tools in general appear rough and basic. They do not often show the decoration which British cabinetmakers in the pre-industrial age often lavished on the wooden stocks and handles.

The Chinese Cabinetmaker's Tools

'The God of the carpenters is Lu Ban
They have to learn the handling of a boatload of tools
Axe, chisel, scraper and drill are always to hand
Square and inkline are studied from their masters
Axe handle, adze stock they make themselves,
Plane blade, gouge and saw cost them money...'
    Pu Songling (1640–1715)[169]

Just as architectural carpenters and cabinetmakers in pre-modern China shared a common legendary patron, and may have shared a common guild organization, so they shared a common repertoire of tools, differentiated according to the fineness of the work under execution. Pu Songling's summary list of tools includes axe, chisel, scraper, drill, adze and plane, in no very systematic order. As a means of dividing the toolkit of the Chinese carpenter into basic types, reference is made to Joseph Needham's classification of mechanical operations necessary for changing the volume and form of matter,[170] though Needham's categories have been re-ordered into those which follow the stages of construction of a piece of wooden furniture.

The problem of terminology here is an acute one. The most observant recorder of China's tool-making tradition, the American scholar Rudolf Hommel carried out invaluable field-work in the 1920s, but failed to give Chinese names for the objects which he illustrated.[171] He may have refrained from doing so due to uncertainty over the status of his informants' terms, many of which were as likely as not regional forms unknown in the standard language. We thus have no account of the variation in names of tools in different parts of China. Nor do we have any account of changing names across time. The terms given below are drawn from a standard modern Chinese manual on woodworking,[172] and may have carried different meanings in earlier centuries. For example, this modern manual and a fifteenth century source are in agreement about the words for axe, saw and chisel, but they differ over the words for scraper and adze.[173]

1) Tools of Cutting

59   Included in this category are saws, axes, adzes, chisels and gouges. The initial stage of turning a log into planks, having stripped it of its bark, was achieved with a two man board or frame saw (*jia ju*). More detailed preparation was carried out with a bow saw of the type illustrated, called a *da ju* or 'great saw'. Back saws or dovetail saws (*jia bei ju*) were also used in the furniture trade. Hommel illustrates two

59 *Chinese carpenter's tools*: bow saw (length 63 cm) '96–40, bow drill '96–41, chisel '96–49, large plane (length 37.5 cm) '96–45, small plane (length 16.5 cm) '96–46, axe (length 41.5 cm) '96–48, Collected in Chongqing, Sichuan province. About 1895. By courtesy of the Trustees of the Museum of Mankind, Given by Sir A.W. Franks.

60 *Chinese carpenter's tools*: bow drill, adze, plane, axle plane, gouges, back saw, chisels. About 1870. By courtesy of the Trustees of the Science Museum.

examples with unusually elaborate carved handles, and quotes an informant to the effect that this tool for the sawing of grooves was 'indispensable for making highgrade hardwood furniture'.

The carpenter's axe (fu) was used in pre-modern times at least as much as an instrument of percussion as of cutting, with the heavy back of the head used in place of any specialized hammer. Indeed this is still often the practice of Chinese cabinetmakers today. One illustration to the Ming editions of the *Classic of Lu Ban* clearly shows a craftsman using the back of his axe to hammer home the leg of a table similar in construction to that shown in 30.[174] According to Hommel, the adze was "not often found" among the carpenter's kit, but the word (ben) does appear in Pu Songling's list. Given its importance as a self-jigging tool, one in which the worked surface acts as a jig so that the next stroke continues in the same level plane,[175] it seems unlikely that adzes played no part at all in the preparation of the level parts of a piece of furniture. A thrusting adze is illustrated in a Ming children's reading book, under the name *chan*. They are also prominent in the repertoire of the traditional Korean cabinetmaker, whose technical resources compare closely with those of his Chinese counterpart.[176]

61   The application of a cutting edge plus percussion is the task of the chisel, both the straight edged chisel (zao) and the curved-bladed gouge (qu zao). These were of course the main tools behind freehand carved decoration, but they also probably played a part in the production of rounded members such as legs and arms, since turning was hardly ever used before the nineteenth century, when it became necessary to produce western-style furniture for foreign residents in China.

61 *Detail* of FE.18–1980.

2) Tools for Scraping

60   Planes and drills are the main tools in this category. The Chinese plan is like the western and unlike the Japanese and Korean versions in that it is pushed away from the user, not pulled towards him. A smoothing plane (ping bao) of a type still in use today can be seen in action in the *Classic of Lu Ban*, with its two handles at right-angles to the blade as in the example illustrated.[177] The rabbit/rebate plane (zi kou bao), its blade exposed at one edge as its Chinese name implies, was used to cut right-angled rebates such as those on the outside frames of table tops, into which the central floating panels would fit. A grooving plane (la bao) was used to cut rectangular grooves set in from the edge of a piece of wood, an adjustable gauge or fence setting the distance from the edge. These could be used for example for cutting the grooves to take the internal shelves of cupboards. A rounding shave, in Chinese

called a *wu bao*, 'bird-plane' (from its appearance like a bird with spread wings), a *zhou bao*, 'axle plane' or a *wan bao*, 'curved plane' was used on members destined to have a circular or oval cross-section. Its slightly concave blade, again pushed away from the user, helped to produce the required profile. Its existence does suggest that the principle of the spokeshave, that is the plane with a blade shaped to cut a particular type of moulding, was known in China. Indeed a spokeshave was probably used to produce the elegant concave moulding seen on all the members of the chairs in 3, as well as the curved profile of the flanges on tables such as those in 38 and 40, and the outside edges of the frames of the tables in 28 and 30. However Hommel does not illustrate such a tool and the utilitarian tone of modern Chinese carpenters' manuals does not put a premium on niceties of design or decoration, though spokeshaves were known and used for detailing in late traditional Korean woodworking.

The reciprocating bow drill played an important part in the cutting of holes for tenons and for dowels. It has been superseded in the modern carpenter's toolkit by the familiar western bib and brace drill. Another tool no longer in use is the 'scraper' (*chan*) on Pu Songling's list. Hommel illustrates one of these wooden holders for nineteen parallel steel blades, and describes its use in smoothing the surface of very hard timbers, those too hard to be workable with a plane. At least some of the historic Chinese cabinet woods come into the category. The tool was in use also among workers in ivory in Shanghai at least until the middle of this century.[178] A metal file (*cuo*) of a different type is shown in the Ming illustrated primer. Abrasion of a much finer degree, necessary in the final finish of hardwood furniture, was provided by the coarse rush *Equisetum hiemale L.*, in Chinese *mu zei*, used by and known to craftsmen in Britain as Dutch rush or scouring rush. This was used to work in the beeswax which, applied in a heated environment, gave the final lustre to the wood surface and brought out the beauty of its grain.

The few illustrations we have of Chinese cabinetmakers at work often show them working on the ground. However simple scaffolds and trestles of undressed logs were used when sawing.

3) Tools of Measurement

62 The toolkit was completed by the basic tools of measurement. Common to all East Asian carpenters is the inked line (*mo dou*), a string which when pulled from its housing is coated in ink before being dropped under tension on to the surface of the timber to provide a guide for cutting. The set-square (*qu chi*), both the T-square

and the L-square were in use in pre-modern China, and were often marked out in inches. The straight foot rule was also employed. The subject of the units of measurement employed in the furniture trade is a complicated one, complicated by the variation in length of the Chinese foot (*chi*) and inch (*cun*) according to regional and historical differences. A Ming 'foot' seems to have been standard at 32 cm, but in the following Qing period it varied from 31 to 35.3 cm. It was not even standard within the same craft tradition, two surviving Qing tailor's rules being respectively 34.9 and 35.8 cm.[179] The 'inches' on the L-square and the foot rule illustrated, tools which were collected in the same place and which come from the same set, are actually of different lengths. Each 'inch' on the L-square is 3.3 cm, while those on the foot rule measure 3.57 cm. This variability makes it unlikely that even a very widely based statistical study of proportion and measurement in Chinese furniture could allow individual pieces to be securely dated or assigned to one area.

62 *Chinese carpenter's measuring tools*: L–square (length 31.9 cm) '96–50, inked line '96–44, foot rule (length 35.7 cm) '96–42. Collected in Chongqing, Sichuan province. About 1895. By courtesy of the Trustees of the Museum of Mankind, Given by Sir A.W. Franks.

Storage Furniture

An Early Ming Lacquered Table with Drawers

The most frequently published, and certainly the earliest piece in the Museum's Chinese furniture collection is a remarkably rare survival, a piece of the highest quality from the early fifteenth century, executed 63 in carved lacquer on a wooden carcass. This is a table with three equal sized drawers beneath its top surface, which carries an inscription dating it to the Xuande reign (1425–1436) of the Ming dynasty. The dating is confirmed by the clear connection of the dragons, phoenixes and flowers which cover its surface to the decoration of smaller objects from the same period. As the only substantial survival, either inside or outside China, of a large piece of lacquered furniture from one of the highpoints of Chinese lacquering, the table has received a good deal of attention in the literature on that craft.[180] It has been less studied in the light of its place in the history of Chinese furniture.

The table is unique not only for its decoration but for its shape. As well as being among the handful of indubitably pre-sixteenth century pieces still extant, it seems to be a rare surviving example of a type of table which was the ancestor of the much more common 'coffer'. It takes little imagination to see the successive stages of development involved. Presumably the simple table came first, to be followed by the table with drawers. The depth of the area beneath the drawers increased over time, and a base was finally added to provide a storage area accessible only when the drawers were fully removed; this is the form of the coffer. The V&A's lacquer table has no base, the drawers providing the only storage. At least one ceramic tomb model exists of a form transitional between this and the coffer proper, a model which dates from the mid-Ming period.[181]

As with the lacquered wood folding armchair of a similar decorative scheme, the lacquered table may well have been made in a workshop under direct imperial control, perhaps even in Peking's famous 'Orchard Workshop' (*Guo yuan chang*), established soon after the transfer of the capital to the north in 1421. It too may have left an imperial palace as an antique some time ago. Certainly the five-clawed dragons (supposed sign of a provenance in the imperial household) with which it is liberally decorated have been mutilated by the removal of one claw on each foot. (This missing claw has been replaced at some stage in the object's history.) The sumptuous carving of the flat upper surface, as well as rendering the piece practically useless for any

purpose such as writing, is unlikely to have needed enhancement by
the usual textile hangings. The assumption has been that the piece has
a ceremonial or religious character, with the drawers used for the
storage of small utensils (they are no more than 10 cm deep) and
incense, the top for the display of sacrificial vessels. This remains no
more than conjecture.

63 *Table with drawers*, carved red lacquer on
a wood core. Xuande reign (1425–1436),
height 79.2 cm, length of top 119.5 cm,
width of top 84.5 cm, FE.6–1973.

The Origins of the Drawer in China

The drawer is so useful that it is easy to overlook the fact that it is a human invention. The furniture of the ancient Egyptians had drawers, but the first mention of them in China does not occur until many centuries later, in the work of the poet Yu Xin (513–581), whose 'Rhapsody on the Mirror' includes the line, 'Set up the dressing case, pull out the mirror drawer.'[182] Here Yu is clearly talking of something like a precursor of the common type of dressing case represented in the Museum's collection.

However early texts which mention large, multi-drawer cabinets significantly associate them with information storage. They make it clear that the categorizing and sorting of documents (or at least the furniture which enabled one to do so) were still novelties in the Song period. There is a story of how the historian Sima Guang (1019–1086), in writing his monumental work *Zi zhi tong jian* ('The Mirror of Government') made use of a specially constructed cabinet by means of which he would rearrange the originally chronological dynastic annals under thematic headings. A similar object was apparently employed in the thirteenth century by Li Renpu, who:

> '... in order to aid his writing, had made ten cabinets of wood. Each cabinet had twenty drawers, marked with the characters of the sexagenary cycle. Whatever came to his attention was entered in these cabinets, arranged in good order by date and in sequence.'[183]

64 *Dressing case, huali* wood. About 1550–1700, height 45.5 cm, length of base 46.7 cm, width of base 32.2 cm, FE.71–1983, Addis Bequest.

The development of such a systematic approach to the handling of knowledge is an important topic in intellectual history, but has no place here. However it is fair to say that in the West as well as in China the appearance of multi-drawer cabinets is closely tied to the storage and sorting of documents, as with a number of surviving fifteenth century European cupboards designed to hold records of property.[184]

One of the most confusing entries in the *Classic of Lu Ban* is that for a plain, high rectangular table with drawers. Hardwood examples of this type are very rare, (and most surviving desks are of a pedestal type made following western designs in the nineteenth century) though they must surely once have been more common, if one is to judge by the almost evangelistic zeal for the drawer as a useful device seen in the writings of Li Yu:

65,66

> 'The drawer is something which the world has long possessed, but which is often taken lightly – some have them, some are ignorant of them and do without. Yet to have them is to be at ease, to be without them is to be fatigued, as they provide the grounds on which one can cope with one's idleness and conceal one's incompetence. The necessities of life for a man of letters, such as paper and knife, inks and glues (none of which he can be without) cannot always be to hand even though one has servants, since they will have their own places for storing them. And yet they are used as much as one's own two hands. I have a testy temperament, and often when I call the boy and he does not come I do the job myself. In the study, to get up on one's feet is invariably a nuisance whatever the distance involved. Yet once you have drawers all the things which you will need in a hurry are contained within – no need to send for them specially. It is as if there were a genie within, which obeys its master's commands, sweeping away and disposing of all old straw and papers as if they were fallen leaves or dust. It performs the labour of keeping the table tidy, temporarily containing anything until it is consigned to the flames. This is what I mean by "a place which copes with idleness and conceals incompetence". I should make it clear that this does not only apply to writing tables. The places where one plays the *qin*, looks at paintings, worships the Buddha or invites guests should all have drawers, since each affair has its own demands, each object its own necessities.'[185]

Coffers

Confusingly, the illustration which accompanies the *Classic of Lu Ban* text describing a table with drawers, of a type which would have gladdened Li Yu's heart, is of a coffer with three drawers and a lower storage compartment.[186] These coffers survive in a number of collections, and must from their sheer size have played a prominent role in Ming and early Qing interiors. They are however something of an enigma, in that little written or graphic evidence survives to show the variety of contexts in which they were used. Even the name by which they were known in their own day is not certain. In the parlance of modern Peking craftsmen, they are generally *men hu chu* 'closed front coffers'. Those with two drawers are also called *lian er chu*, 'two-in-a-line' coffers, while those with three drawers are, logically, *lian san chu*, 'three-in-a-line coffers'.[187] These names have not so far been identified in early sources.

The reason for the silence about pieces of furniture such as the coffer on the part of writers like Wen Zhenheng and Li Yu is their lack of interest in domestic storage of clothes and everyday utensils. This was the domain of women and servants. Only the storage and display of books and artworks were thought worthy of attention by male writers. We can assume therefore that the coffers were not used for these more glamorous purposes, but for storage of bulky items, which could be put away in the relatively inaccessible lower compartment; items such as bedding, textile hangings for special occasions, perhaps winter clothes as well. They may also have been used for family Buddhist worship and in the cult of ancestors; photographs of temples occasionally show them there too, bearing candlesticks and incense burners.[188] Wen Zhenheng speaks of 'Buddha coffers and Buddha tables', which he asserts must be of black or red lacquer, including carved red lacquer.[189] Lacquered coffers are very much rarer than hardwood ones, though isolated examples do exist, a rarity which is hard to explain given the much larger number of surviving lacquer wardrobes and upright cupboards.

7,68   The Museum's two coffers are very typical of the types. The differences between them lie in the configuration of drawers, the degree of decoration applied to the curving aprons, and the elaboration of the decorative spandrels on the outer sides of the front legs. On the larger coffer these take the form of elaborate openwork carving of snarling dragons. Underlying similarities of detail between the two pieces are if anything just as striking, and point up the remarkable homogeneity of workshop practice across time and space prevailing in the 'classic' period of hardwood furniture from about 1550 to 1750. A

69   comparison of the profiles of the flaring flanges at either end of the tops, of the degree of overhang of the top over the legs, of the outline

69 *Detail* of FE.73–1977, showing openwork spandrel.

Opposite

65 *Desk, huali* wood. About 1850–1900, height 80 cm, length of top 141 cm, width of top 64 cm, FE.22–1980.

66 *Desk, hongmu* wood. About 1850–1900, height 85 cm, length of top 156.5 cm, width of top 65.5 cm, FE.3–1971.

83

of the central portion of the two aprons and the curving, beaded-edged frames of the drawer front shows, if not identical treatments, at least a consensus between two different makers as to the major outlines of the type.

Although, as has been seen, hardwood chairs could have metal fittings in the form of joint-strengthening straps, it is on storage furniture that metalwork, in the form of lockplates, hinges, handles and drawer-pulls, becomes of major significance. Both coffers are designed to have locking drawers, a fact which reveals something about the perceived value of the objects stored in them. The locks are not integral, but would have been separate padlocks. A sliding rectangular plate slots upwards into a groove cut in the wood of the drawer to form a tube through which the pin of the padlock is passed. The brass lockplates on both coffers have a lobed outline, with simple curving or rectangular handles. As is commonly the case, these fittings are later replacements.

71   A small cabinet or coffer on which not only is the metalwork of modern date, but where the whole object has fallen under suspicion, has a flanged top like the two previous examples, but with two doors beneath its drawers. This piece is clearly constructed from timber which once formed part of a much larger cabinet of some type. The pieces of wood forming the frame of the top are disproportionately large for the size of the whole object, while the upper right-hand corner of the door on the left clearly shows the quarter-circle of discolouration caused by a large circular hinge or lockplate. The dismemberment and reconstruction of pieces of furniture has been going on for centuries. These signs are not necessarily indicative of a modern date for the present appearance of the object, though this cannot be ruled out.

70

71

Opposite

67 *Coffer*, *huali* wood. About 1550–1600, height 90 cm, length of top 170 cm, width of top 57 cm, FE.118–1978.

68 *Coffer*, *huali* wood. About 1550–1650, height 81.5 cm, length of top 190 cm, width of top 53 cm, FE.73–1977.

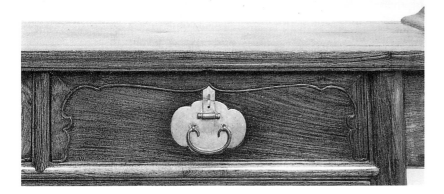

70 *Detail* of FE.118–1978, showing lockplate.

Some Categories of Cupboard

71 This small coffer, originally one of a pair, is nevertheless of value as the only representative within the collection to date of a piece of furniture with wooden pinned doors. One of the many useful distinctions advanced by Wang Shixiang in his classification of Chinese furniture is that between the 'square cornered cabinet' and the 'round cornered cabinet'.[190] The former has vertical sides with doors mounted on external metal hinges, while the latter has sides which slope inwards towards the top, and doors which swing on wooden pegs which are of
72 one piece with the frame of the door panel. A detail of a peg from the door of the small coffer is shown in the photograph. This fits into circular holes in the top and bottom of the door frame, holes which are left 'open' on one side at the bottom only to allow the door to be removed when it is opened to its fullest extent. Also removable is the central bar between the doors, held in place at the bottom by a tenon open on one side.

The true 'round cornered cabinet' is not represented in the Museum's collection as yet. The type is described in the *Classic of Lu Ban* simply as an *yi chu* 'clothes cupboard', though once again there is a poor fit between text and illustration.[191] Something very similar appears in the fifteenth century illustrated primer under the broad category *chu* 'cupboard'.[192]

72 *Detail* of FE.16–1980, showing wooden pin from door hinge.

71 *Small coffer*, one of a pair, *huali* wood. Possibly a twentieth century assembly from earlier components, height 78.5 cm, length of top 97.5 cm, width of top 49.7 cm, FE.16–1980.

The usual confusion of terminology reigns over the history of the two modern Chinese words for cupboard, *chu* and *gui*. For Wang Shixiang the distinction is purely a regional one; *chu* is the southern word and *gui* the northern for what is essentially the same thing. However the indubitably southern *Classic of Lu Ban* employs *chu* for a cupboard with sloping sides and *gui* for one with vertical sides. The fifteenth century illustrated primer has a different distinction, *chu* being again a sloping sided upright cupboard, but *gui* being illustrated by a strange square coffer of a type now unknown.[193] Li Yu uses *chu gui* as one word, and is uncharacteristically casual in his lack of concern for details. Storage is just not an interesting subject for him:

> 'There is no special knowledge or ingenuity in setting up
> coffers and cupboards – their value lies in their holding a lot
> and being good at storing things. Sometimes their construction
> is massive and their capacity very small, which is not so good
> as diminishing the outer form in order to expand the interior.'

He goes on to advocate the fitting of removable shelves as a way of maximizing storage space, and then returns to his old theme of drawers, 'the more you have the better'. He discusses a multi-drawer cabinet, which he describes as being based on the pharmacist's 'hundred-eye cabinet' *bai yan chu*, but for the use of scholars, who thereby save the time normally spent in looking for pieces of information and can spend it on actual composition.[194] A lacquered medicine cabinet from the Wanli period (1576–1619) preserved in the Palace Museum Peking, is a rare (if miniature) survivor of the kind of thing Li Yu had in mind.[195]

Wen Zhenheng employs the word *chu* for all types of cupboard. He is in favour of very large objects, 'the wider the more antique', though he does not favour cupboards with legs unless they have a separate platform or base, rather like a *kang* table. Some of the *kang* tables surviving in collections may in fact have started life as platforms for cabinets, platforms described as *chu dian* by Wen. The kind of

73 cupboard in question may have resembled those illustrated, a pair with lower storage sections and upper display sections, 'suitable for the display of antique bronzes, jades and curios' as he puts it.[196] Just as with paintings, the three-dimensional objects in a late Ming connoisseur's collection would not have been on permanent display, but would have been shown in rotation according to season and mood. The bulk of the collection would have remained at any one time in individual boxes, locked in the cabinet's lower sections.

74 The brass fittings of these cabinets are relatively modern replacements, and again there is considerable evidence that at least
75,76 some of the timber is reused. Filled-in mortises and, on the back, the

75 *Detail* of FE.14–1980, showing filled mortise.

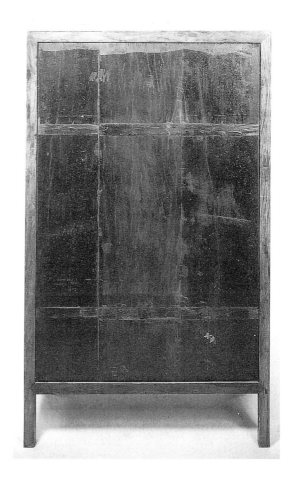

73 *Cupboard*, one of a pair, *huali* wood. About 1600–1700, height 122.5 cm, length of top 74.5 cm, width of top 43.5 cm, FE.14–1980.

76 *Rear* of FE.14–1980.

74 *Detail* of FE.14–1980, showing lockplate.

horizontal signs of dovetailed braces, which suggest the back panels may have once been part of a table top, confirm this.

The development of such combined storage and display units in the eighteenth century is illustrated by a highly elaborate lacquered wood set of shelves. The piece has a detachable base, and is decorated in carved red lacquer, painted polychrome lacquer and gold-on-black lacquer of a loosely Japanese inspiration. There is a considerable body of evidence for Chinese knowledge and appreciation of Japanese lacquer in the sixteenth, seventeenth and eighteenth centuries, both as regards forms and styles of decoration. In its boldly asymmetrical arrangement of shelves this cabinet is loosely based on the Japanese *tana*, a type of furniture known from literary evidence to have been imported into China and admired there at least from the late Ming.[197]

The Museum lacks an example of furniture designed purely for the storage of books, and no examples survive anywhere of the huge shelves, 7 'feet' high and 14 'feet' broad specified by Wen Zhenheng. His advice to avoid putting books on the bottom shelf, where they will be spoiled by damp, is revealing of the expected standards of comfort in even the grandest Ming homes.[198] Books and antiques are the only possessions whose storage interests him, his lack of concern for the storage of other things being paralleled by the absence of tomb models of cupboards and coffers from all the major excavated Ming sites detailed in the notes (though isolated examples have been seen on the art market).

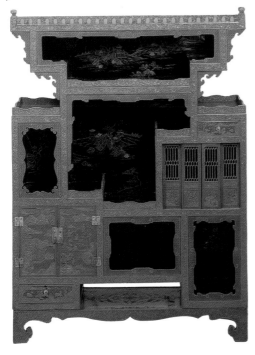

77 *Display cabinet*, carved red lacquer and painted lacquer on a wood core. About 1730–1780, height 116 cm, length 84 cm, width 28.5 cm, FE.56–1983, Given by the Museums and Galleries Commission from the estate of Mrs L. F. Palmer.

78 *Clothes chest*, camphor wood. About 1820–1880, height 92 cm, length 169 cm, width 77.2 cm, FE.77–1983, Addis Bequest.

The *Classic of Lu Ban*, from the maker's point of view, is more forthcoming. It gives full specifications for a type of chest with a hinged lid which it calls an *yi long*, 'clothes chest', with a detachable base. The *Classic of Lu Ban* seems to employ the terms *long* and *xiang* interchangeably for 'chest'. The Song dynasty writer Dai Tong noted that these terms were only coming into use in his time, replacing the older words *qie* and *si*. To him a *long* was deeper than a *xiang*, a distinction largely lost by the Ming period.[199.] The change in terminology may be related to the development of chests with hinged lids, rather than the earlier type of clothes storage boxes with detachable lids fitting over a riser, such as are seen in the famous second century BC tombs at Mawangdui.

78   The Museum's example of this form is made of camphor wood, often employed in whole or in part for the manufacture of furniture designed to contain textiles, due to its insect repellent qualities. It has the removable base (*chejiao*, literally 'cart base') and retains its massive brass padlock. Though this example is not earlier than the nineteenth century, this simplest of furniture forms has changed very little since the sixteenth century, and a ceramic model of very similar proportions has been excavated from a tomb of the mid-seventeenth.[200] It is the low relief carved decoration of the base which in this case is sufficient to establish a late-Qing date.

Straight-seamed Chinese garments, their folds often perfumed with the aroma from openwork tubular perfume holders, were never hung vertically but always laid in chests or on shelves.[201] This could involve cupboards of very large size, such as those observed in a Canton household in 1556 by the Portuguese Dominican Gaspar da Cruz:

> 'Entering in the first of these houses (which is large) it has
> therein some huge cupboards very well wrought and carved,
> but the work is more for strength and durability than for show.
> They have likewise chairs with shoulder backs, all made of a
> very strong wood and very well made, in such wise that their
> furniture is durable and of great repute and credit, which
> endures for their sons and grandsons.'[202]

This, the first western notice of Chinese hardwood furniture, reveals that these large storage cupboards sometimes stood in the forward reception rooms of a house to which visitors might be admitted, an arrangement still to be seen in the imperial palace in Peking, where the Hall of Supreme Harmony houses a pair of truly monumental cupboards. An encyclopaedia of useful knowledge for the householder, published around 1600, says that cupboards should never be placed against the back wall of a room (i.e. they should not face you as you enter the room but should always stand against the side walls).[203]

While not of quite such a size as the palace pair, the Museum's imposing pair of clothes cupboards in hardwood, dating from around 1600, are still by far the largest pieces of furniture in the collection, at well over eight feet high. Ladders were needed to reach objects stored in the separate upper compartment. To Wang Shixiang, these are *chao yi gui*, 'court dress cupboards'. Their great width, the removable central door post and the removable outer panels of the doors (*yu sai ban*), on rigid tenons at the top but held in only by removable pegs at the bottom, all make for ease of maneuvering stiff and heavy silk garments onto the camphor wood shelves. The upper portion (*ding xiang*) was used for the storage of boots, headgear and other smaller accessories. According to Wang, such a pair of cupboards can also be called a *si jian da gui*, 'four-part great cabinet', from the two lower and two separate upper sections which make up the complete ensemble.[204]

This particular pair is distinguished not only by the fine state of preservation, which extends to the rough coat of composition and lacquer on the unseen back and top surfaces, but by the survival of the original brass metalwork, chased with designs of butterflies and dragons. These dragons are echoed in the carving of the apron, where two winged monsters confront one another against a background of motifs, originally Buddhist in inspiration but now employed purely as space-fillers, called the 'eight precious emblems'. It is the stylistic

80 *Detail* of FE.73–1983, showing hinge.

91

79 *Pair of cupboards, huali* wood. About 1550–1620, height 263 cm, length 62.5 cm, width 157 cm, FE.73 & FE.74–1983, Addis Bequest.

82 *Cupboard*, one of a pair, painted and inlaid lacquer on a wood core. About 1650–1700, height 181 cm, length 96 cm, width 63.8 cm, W.24–1939, Edward Lawrence Cockell Bequest.

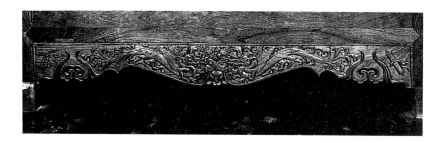

81 *Detail* of FE.73–1983, showing apron.

similarities between these panels and the chronologically more secure body of Chinese porcelain decoration which enables a slightly less nebulous date to be advanced in this case.

82 A pair of cupboards of a radically different aesthetic, though perhaps only thirty or forty years later in date, are executed in a variety of lacquering techniques, the most striking being the inlay of a variety of semi-precious and coloured stones, which stand out in relief from the black surface. This technique, known as 'Zhou work' (*Zhou zhi*) after a supposed inventor named Zhou Zhu, appears to have been developed in the late sixteenth century, the first textual reference to it being in 1594.[205] It was practised on hardwood as well as on lacquered surfaces, a notable example of the former style being a pair of wardrobes in the Metropolitan Museum of Art, New York.[206] Here on the V&A pair of cupboards the decoration on the lower sections is the popular subject of a collection of antiques and curios, while the upper sections show the equally common theme of women and children playing in a garden, suggesting an original placement for the cupboards in the women's section of the house. This theme continues upwards on to the fronts of the hinged tops. The upper sections are

83 fitted with handles, which should remind us that storage furniture too was designed for portability. In an episode from the mid-seventeenth century novel *A Marriage to Astonish the Age*, a divorced wife packs her belongings into a *gui* (i.e. a vertical wardrobe rather than a horizontal chest) which is then removed by being strapped to carrying poles.[207] The cabinet might well have been part of the original marriage settlement along with the clothes it contained, hence its return to the

84 woman's parental home. The sides of both cupboards are decorated, in painted lacquer and oil paint, with floral subjects in square and circular frames. These provide a date before which the cabinets cannot have been made, since they follow closely some of the plates in later editions of *Shizhu zhai shu hua pu* ('The Ten Bamboo Studio Manual of Painting and Calligraphy), which began to be issued in 1627.[208] The use here of printed designs for furniture decoration is not unique. Indeed two separate graphic sources could be used on the opposing doors of one and the same lacquered cupboard.[209]

94

83 *Detail* of W.24–1939.

84 *Detail* of W.24–1939.

86 *Cupboard*, gilded red lacquer on a wood core. About 1850–1900, height 181.3 cm, length 155.1 cm, width 67.5 cm, W.33–1932, Given by W.E. Blake.

The technique of high-relief inlay in furniture, also known as *bai bao kan* 'hundred precious things inlay', was to remain a popular one throughout the Qing dynasty. It received a boost in workshops in Peking earlier this century, when numerous fakes in the style of the pair discussed above were produced. A lavishly decorated cupboard which entered the Museum as recently as 1968, though described at the time as a 'handsome piece' in 'a rare class', and as being of the Kangxi period (1664–1722), now appears likely to have been made in Peking in the 1930s, where it was originally purchased. It may well be a product of the only workshop which can now be identified, that of Zhang Gui.[210]

85

86   Of similar date but more modest pretentions is a cupboard in a distinctive style which has been located to the province of Zhejiang, on the south bank of the lower Yangtze. It is decorated in gold on red lacquer, the gold being used to pick out the low relief carving of flowers, curios and theatrical scenes. It demonstrates the survival into our own times, in the furniture made for more modest rural homes, of a vernacular version of 'high' decorative taste and a once-elegant decorative repertoire.

85 *Cupboard*, painted and inlaid black lacquer on a wood core. About 1930, height 163.2 cm, length 99.5 cm, width 40.7 cm, W.5–1968.

Dressing Cases and Other Storage

87
88
Storage had to be provided for other necessities of life, as well as for clothes. Small dressing cases to contain cosmetics, toiletries, jewellery and the combs and mirrors needed by both men and women survive in some numbers in both lacquered wood and hardwood from the Ming and Qing periods. Varying as they do in size, they point up the essentially artificial nature of the western category 'furniture', which has tended to include the hardwood examples and exclude the lacquered examples of what is in essence the same thing. Perhaps a more real distinction is between those with a solid life-off front, which may be the earlier type, and those with hinged doors. In both types the top is hinged, and can act as a stand for the mirror when wedged open. Such dressing cases are often seen in book illustration, usually in women's apartments, and are referred to in the *Classic of Lu Ban* as *jing xiang*, 'mirror caskets'.[211] One more colloquial name for them is *guan pi xiang*, a term of uncertain etymology which can be written in more than one way but which certainly cannot be used to support the name 'seal chest' by which they have become known in the West.

88 *Dressing case*, FE.71–1983.

87 *Dressing case*, polychrome inlaid lacquer on a wood core. Jiajing reign (1522–1566), height 25.4 cm, length of base 28.2 cm, width of base 18.6 cm, FE.88–1974, Given by Sir Harry Garner and Lady Garner.

89 *Chest for ice*, *huali* and *hongmu* woods with lead lining. About 1700–1850, height 77.5 cm, top 64.5 x 64.5 cm, FE.113–1981.

One distinctively Chinese form of storage occasionally encountered is in the form of chests for ice, a necessary coolant at the height of the hot and humid Chinese summer. Ice was stored during the winter in subterranean pits, to be broken up and kept in special chests during hot weather. These chests are found in enamelled metal as well as, in this case, in lead-lined hardwood, and were sometimes used without their accompanying stands, set under dining tables to cool those sitting at them. The unusually sturdy handles enable this very heavy chest (which must have been even heavier when filled with ice) to be moved to the place of greatest need.

Heating in the pre-modern Chinese house, as well as relying on the *kang*, the brick platform mentioned above, was dependent on free standing mobile braziers burning coal or charcoal. Obviously these were not made of wood due to the fire risk, and so are not generally treated as 'furniture'. Examples of large metal braziers are rare, but their importance can be learned from literature. The Chinese interior could be a chilly place, where it was perfectly natural to have to breathe on an inkstone in order to unfreeze the water sufficiently for ink to be ground, and where the inevitable corollary of being warm enough was air whirling with soot, a 'world of ashes' as Li Yu put it.[212] An important practical adjunct which also had an important decorative function was the screen. These came in a variety of sizes and forms, the most elegant in Wen Zhenheng's eyes being single-panel screens inlaid with slabs of marble. He dismisses folding screens in general,[213] though this is the type most commonly represented in western collections, often in the form of the large presentation screens in incised lacquer which have been an object of admiration since they first reached the west in the seventeenth century.

Light too was a problem, just how much of a problem it is hard to grasp from the glare of an electric age. Most purposeful and most social activity in Ming and Qing China took place in daylight, and a feast that required lanterns was likely to be a vaguely improper, all-male affair with entertainers and noisy drinking games. Lampshades of paper, oxhorn or (in the Qing) very thin porcelain shaded the light of wax candles, set sometimes on the top of hardwood lampstands with poles of adjustable height.

90 *Lamp stand, huali* wood (the pole a modern replacement). About 1650–1750, height 135 cm, length of base 30 cm, width of base 36.5 cm, FE.5–1971.

Traditional Chinese Furniture in the Modern World

In 1970, in the context of an exhibition surveying the chair in Europe since 1900, the question could legitimately be posed; 'Has the chair a future'[214] Nearly twenty years later it seems more of a period piece, a reminder of an era when the future course of design seemed to tend towards 'environments' and away from the free standing piece of furniture as autonomous artefact. The chair is still with us, its possibilities far from exhausted. Or rather, chairs are still with us, since the prescriptive functionalism which could seek to bring history to a close by christening Hans Wegner's beech and cane dining chair of 1949 'The Chair'[215] has given way to pluralist exploration of material, technique, profitability and stylishness. It is a good time therefore for designers to examine the products of the major non-European furniture tradition, that of China.

Another factor is propitious for such an enterprise. Adolf Loos's 1908 equation of 'Ornament' with 'Crime' has lost its spell, its power to throw a functionalist veil over our perceptions.[216] The Western literature on Chinese furniture has been, at least since the 1940s, permeated with a veneration for one strand within that tradition, the type of minimally decorated object executed solely in hardwood timber, where the effect is achieved solely through the deployment of certain geometrically simple forms. Furniture in which 'decoration' plays a major part, through carving, inlaying or the lacquering of the finished surface, has been by contrast held in lower esteem. Such prejudices need have no place in a design culture which is now frankly post-functionalist. Ornament is no longer a crime.

By viewing lacquered and wooden furniture as a totality, not as two opposing entities, we are at one with at least some of the consumers of such furniture, the Chinese writers on taste and style whose work has been presented above. These arbiters of elegance set up several categories of opposition in their writings; between northern and southern, between 'vulgar' and 'elegant', between fashionable and unfashionable. At no point in any piece of pre-modern Chinese writing on interior design is there evidence that the hardwood furniture so admired today enjoyed unequivocally or consistently higher esteem than furniture in other materials. In fact, as we have seen, there is evidence to the contrary.

In opposition to modern western and Chinese attempts to supply rational criteria for aesthetic pronouncements, whether phrased in terms of 'form and function' or by appeal to the principles of ergonomics (the scientific study of the human frame), these Chinese authors, contemporaries of many of the artefacts discussed above, are frankly irrational. They invoke now-mysterious tides of taste and fashion they praise and condemn on the basis of distinctions too fine to be discernible to us today. Their language about stylishness and acceptability was one they may or may not have shared with the makers of the furniture, but it is certainly one from a full appreciation of which we are now irrevocably excluded. If we take functionalism as our guide in the study of a culture where the polemical lines were just as sharply drawn as in our own, but drawn in a different direction over different ground, all we shall discover are reflections of our own prejudices.

It is by now traditional to decry, in any piece of work on Chinese furniture, the lack of attention the subject has received from both Chinese and western writers. In fact one might argue that hardwood furniture has received *too much* attention, having been the subject of several monographs in English, at least one recent Ph.D. thesis in the United States and an increasing number of articles in Chinese, culminating in Wang Shixiang's magisterial, *Classic Chinese Furniture*. Through all this material runs the assumption that hardwood furniture is a subject worthy of study on its own, a coherent sub-division of Chinese material culture. Yet the fact that we see it as such should not lead us to accept that it was so viewed in centuries before our own. It is not simply élite snobbishness about the products of the artisan which limits the amount of space given to furniture in traditional writing on taste. There is quite simply no pre-modern generic Chinese word for furniture. The modern world, *jiaju*, has had the meaning only in relatively recent times, its literal meaning 'household implements', being originally applied to agricultural implements. In the sixteenth and seventeenth centuries 'chairs and tables' existed, 'furniture' did not.

If the whole concept of 'furniture' as an autonomous category in Chinese culture is suspect, the arbitrary isolation of 'Ming hardwood furniture' is even more so. Although interest in early furniture was reviving among Chinese connoisseurs in Peking in the early part of this century,[217] the creation of the category owes much to western writers. In the course of this creation, the very words 'Chinese furniture' have changed their meaning. In 1922, in the course of a full-blooded revival of *chinoiserie* taste in France, Odilon Roche could entitle a book *Les meubles de la Chine*, and yet include in its fifty-four plates examples of lacquered furniture only. Lacquered furniture *was* 'Chinese furniture' then, but it was already being discussed in terms of 'vigorous simplicity', as an art 'of which the dominant qualities were simplicity, nobility and grandeur'. Despite his mistaken belief that Chinese furniture 'is rarely in plain wood', Roche did stress the simplicity of its forms.[218] The English translation of Roche's pioneering work, with an independent introduction by Herbert Cescinsky, based its discussion on the opposition, familiar in British debate about the applied arts of Japan and China, between 'mechanical perfection' and 'artistic spirit'. Ceskinsky implicitly denigrated the Japanese lacquers so admired by the previous generation, contrasting them with the Chinese pieces in Roche's plates. He claims that in these Chinese pieces, 'form receives far less attention than actual decoration', without explicitly identifying this as a weakness. He also offers the view that very little Ming furniture had survived, his datings being accordingly conservative by present standards.[219]

In a volume published in 1927 continuing Roche's format, Marcel Dupont was the first western author to make plain his assumption that plain equals early, that increasing decoration is a sign of a late, and implicitly decadent taste.[220] Dupont's equation, which now has penetrated the general consciousness of many, finds however no echo in the interesting American interior decorating literature of the 1930s, where several articles make a feature of Chinese furniture as part of the elegant interior. The emphasis in these pieces, written by journalists and hence revealing something of the general educated western perception of Chinese furniture at the time, is on 'gold and red lacquer', or 'ancient Ningpo carving'. The furniture visible in the photographs would now generally be ascribed to the eighteenth and nineteenth centuries, and indeed is so dated by one author. No attempt is made to put a Ming date on pieces, and the language used about them betrays a continuing interest in exoticism rather than in their supposedly 'modern' resonances.[221]

The first overt application of the western term 'functionalism' appears in an American journal of 1940:

> 'While at the same time Chinese craftsmen were creating
> ornate and rococo furniture, they were also quite familiar with
> what modernists call functionalism. Hence many pieces of
> antique Chinese furniture can be combined harmoniously with
> modern interiors.'[222]

What is interesting about this quote is that it refers to a pair of stools and a table which are *decorated* in an ornate surface lacquer technique, and which are quite properly dated by the anonymous author to the eighteenth century. Thus were there was at this point no connection made between prestigious 'functionalism' and plain hardwood furniture, nor with a supposed date in the Ming dynasty. That was to come within a few years.

To John C. Ferguson, writing his *Survey of Chinese Art* in China in 1940, there was no doubt that 'The greatest development of artistic furniture in China took place in the Ming dynasty...' even if the Palace Museum 'contains almost all of the Ming dynasty furniture which has been preserved'. In his discussion of individual pieces he gives equal weight to pieces in undecorated wood and in lacquered wood.[223] The big leap into an exclusive definition of the subject was to come four years later, when the German professor at one of Peking's foreign-run universities, Gustav Ecke brought out (in an extremely limited edition of 200 copies) his *Chinese Domestic Furniture*. Despite its title this is a study, an admirable and pioneering study, of what is nevertheless only one part of the domestic furniture of China. Ecke simply ignored lacquer furniture; at a stroke it became unworthy of notice. His language is the language of morality. Hardwood furniture is 'free from pretence', it manifests 'purity' and 'respect for organic substance'. His model of development is an organic one, with much talk of 'flourishing' and 'decline', in which the Ming dynasty is an indisputable highpoint and in which the only secure dating criterion is that the 'better' pieces are the earlier ones. Ecke ends with a frankly romantic evocation of a Ming dynasty 'home of the ruling class', where the 'amber or purple hues of rosewood pieces' play a major part in an ambiance of austere, dignified luxury.[224] The imaginative force of Ecke's writing, coupled with its acuity on many points such as the origins of the chair and the identifications for the first time of many of the hardwood timbers, and with its excellent plates and plans, have given *Chinese Domestic Furniture* a classic and unassailed status. Without questioning Ecke's achievement as the author of the first serious monograph on a part of the Chinese furniture tradition, a look at what the inhabitants of the Ming ruling class interior said at the time can only challenge Ecke's conclusion that hardwood furniture is or ever was the *only* 'Chinese furniture'.

Though Ecke's writing can hardly have enjoyed a wide circulation initially, the views he propounded were shared by a circle of western residents in China and rapidly became part of the common currency of discussion. In 1946 the hardwood furniture of the brothers William and Robert Drummond was shown at the Baltimore Museum of Art. Accompanying publicity assumed that visitors to the exhibition would be:

> '... surprised to find a group of objects amazingly modern in
> their emphasis on functional structure. Instead of the perhaps
> expected and all too well known works of ornate lacquer
> and elaborately carved teakwood he will be confronted with
> pieces distinguished by simplicity of design, purity and
> elegance of line and beauty of the natural wood.'[225]

Four years after that George Kates could without irony contrast the 'Ming' hardwood pieces in his *Chinese Household Furniture* (another seemingly all-embracing but actually exclusive title) with the 'bad taste of the Victorian age' and its fondness for the merely ornate. There is an opposition in his thought between 'functional' and 'decorated', as well as an expression of the common view of China as somehow moving at a slower pace than a more dynamic West:

> 'We are not dealing with an ever–changing, inconstant
> fashion, but with discreet and intelligent variation upon a
> single noble theme ...'[226]

Kates may well have been right in his insistence that the Chinese élite in the late nineteenth and early twentieth centuries admired and exalted the plainer, hardwood furniture. Operating as he was with a model of an essentially stagnant China, and in ignorance of any of the Ming textual evidence, he could only assume that the tastes of the late traditional society in which he, Ecke, Drummond and their contemporaries had chosen to move had hardly changed in four hundred years.

By 1955, a revealing brief article on the reproduction furniture business carried out in New York by the Drummond brothers referred to the type of original hardwood furniture in which they had originally dealt simply as 'Ming furniture'.[227] The writings of Robert Ellsworth, particularly the highly valuable *Chinese Furniture; Hardwood Examples of the Ming and early Ch'ing Dynasties* can relegate the qualification to the subtitle, for by then, in a total reversal of the situation prevailing fifty years before, hardwood furniture *was* 'Chinese furniture'. Even the first attempt in many years, perhaps significantly by a Frenchman, to include all types of material within the covers of the same book treats the hardwood and lacquer traditions as separate categories to be confined within separate chapters.[228] A contemporary American writer can dismiss the contribution of lacquered furniture to the dating of hardwood furniture on the grounds that it, 'belongs to a different tradition' and is 'much more ornate'. These grounds are noteworthy in that they relate to the problem of dating hardwood furniture, as being the overriding concern of any study of the material. It is the same author who 'assumes that the pieces (discussed) were not made after the fall of the Ming dynasty because of their high technical and aesthetic quality.'[229] The assumption here is not a small one, and the burden of proof must lie with its proponents.

The Victoria and Albert Museum's collection of Chinese furniture, with its wide variation in type, material, date of manufacture and of acquisition, can perhaps fruitfully be used to approach a less narrow view of one of the world's major furniture traditions. The very difficult nature of some of the problems the collection poses can act as a spur to further investigation, which will take as its starting point the interrelation of material, textual and pictorial evidence. A truly definitive account of Chinese furniture will never be possible, because the set of questions put forward by the surviving, as well as the lost, body of material bears upon the whole of our understanding of traditional Chinese culture. It is in these connections between material culture and the wider sphere which gives it meaning that the true value of a study such as this is hoped to lie.

Notes

1 Texts used: Huang Bosi, *Yan ji tu* and Ge Shan, *Die ji tu* ('Illustrations of the Folding Table'), in one volume together with Zhu Qiqian, *Kuang ji tu* ('Illustrations of Shelving') and printed as *Cun su tang jiao xie ji pu san zhong* ('Three Annotated and Illustrated Texts on Furniture from the Hall where Plainness Resides') (Peking, 1933 reprinted Shanghai, 1983).

2 The remarks on furniture are contained within the 'Discourse on the Elegant Enjoyment of Pleasurable Idleness', the sixth of the *Eight Discourses*. It is printed as a separate text: Gao Lian, *Yan xian qing shang jian* ('Discourse on the Elegant Enjoyments of Leisure'), Meishu congshu, san ji dishi ji (Shanghai, 1936), the version employed here.

3 The relevant sections are separately printed: Tu Long, *Qi ju qi fu jian* ('Notes on Utensils and Clothing for Daily Life'), Meishu congshu er ji dijiu ji (Shanghai, 1936).

4 The punctuated and annotated text employed here is Wen Zhenheng, *Zhang wu zhi jiao zhu* ('The Treatise on Superfluous Things, Edited and Annotated'), with notes by Chen Zhi (Nanjing, 1984).

5 L. Carrington Goodrich and Donald L. Potter, 'Wen Chenmeng' in *Dictionary of Ming Biography*, edited by L. Carrington Goodrich and Chaoying Fang, 2 vols (New York and London, 1976), II, 1467–1471. Charles O. Hucker, 'Su-chou and the Agents of Wei Chung-hsien, 1626' in Charles O. Hucker, *Two Studies in Ming History*, Michigan Papers in Chinese Studies no 12 (Ann Arbor, 1971), pp.41–83.

6 Wen Zhenheng, p.225.

7 The section on interior design printed separately: Li Yu, *Yi jia yan ju shi qi wan bu* ('The Section on Dwellings and Utensils from The Words of One Master'), in one volume together with Li Dou, *Gong duan ying zao lu* ('A Record of Architectural Regulations') (Peking, 1931 reprinted Shanghai, 1983).

8 Liu Dunzhen, 'Lu Ban ying zao zheng shi', (Lu Ban's Orthodox Types of Architecture'), *Wenwu* (1962.2), 7–11.

9 Wang Shixiang, 'Lu Ban jing jiang jia jing jiaju tiaokuan chu shi' ('An Explanation of the Entries on Furniture in *The Classic of Lu Ban and the Craftsman's Mirror*'), Part I, *Gugong bowuyuan yuankan* (1980.3), 55–68; Part II, *Gugong bowuyuan yuankan* (1981.1), 74–89.

10 A point firsr propounded by Dr Frances Wood.

11 Zhou Shilin, *Tian shui bing shan lu* ('A Record of the Waters of Heaven Melting the Iceberg'), Zhi bu zu zhai congshu ed. (1790).

12 Wei Meiyue, 'Qingdai Qianlong shiqi Junjichu dang youguan chaojia dang'an zhi shiliao ji qi jiazhi' ('The value of archival records of household confiscations in the archives of the Grand Council from the Qianlong period'), *Gugong jikan* 15.1 (1980), 1–41.

13 e.g. Wen Zhenheng's chapter on 'Arrangement', *wei zhi*, pp.347–349.

14 Principally Louise Hawley Stone, *The Chair in China* (Toronto, 1952). C. P. Fitzgerald, *Barbarian Beds: the Origin of the Chair in China* (London, 1965). Wu Tung, 'From Imported Nomadic Seat to Chinese Folding Armchair', *Bulletin of the Museum of Fine Arts Boston*, 71 (1973), 36–51. Jan Chapman, 'Back to the hu ch'uang-a reassessment of some evidence concerning the origin of the chair in China', *Oriental Art*, New Series, 20 (1974), 425–430. Chen Zengbi, 'Lun Handai wu zhuo' (On the lack of high tables in the Han period), *Kaogu yu wenwu* (1982.5), 91–97. Yi Shui, 'Man hua hu chuang-jiaju tan wang zhi san' (Notes on the huchuang – topics in furniture no 3), *Wenwu* (1982.10), 82–85. Ole Wanscher, *Sella Curulis: the Folding Stool, an Ancient Symbol of Dignity* (Copenhagen, 1980), pp.279–290.

15 Sergei I. Rudenko, *Frozen Tombs of Siberia, the Pazyryk Burials of Iron Age Horsemen*, translated and edited by Dr D. W. Thompson (London, 1970), p.326, pl.154.

16 *Nan Qi shu* ('The Book of the Southern Qi'), Zhonghua shuju ed., 3 vols (Peking, 1972), I, 986.

17 *Nihon no bukkyō o kizuita hitobito-sono shōzō to sho / Special Exhibition of Buddhist Portraiture*, Nara National Museum (Nara, 1981), pls. 59, 60, 61.

18 Wu Tung, fig. 3.

19 He Zicheng, 'Tang mu bihua' ('Tang tomb murals'), *Wenwu*, 1959.8, 31–33 (p.33).

20 Edwin O. Reischauer, *Ennin's Diary, The Record of a Pilgrimage to China in Search of the Law* (New York, 1955), pp.50, 52 & 111.

21 The principal excavations with evidence for the early history of Chinese furniture, together with approximate dates, are: 'Jiangsu Hanjiang Caizhuang Wudai mu qingli jianbao' (Report on a Five Dynasties tomb at Caizhuang, Hanjiang country, Jiangsu province), *Wenwu* (1980.8), 41–51 (10th century wooden model couch, stools and clothes rack). Chen Zengbi, 'Qian nian gu ta' (A thousand year old couch), *Wenwu*

(1984.6), 66–69 (10th century full size model). 'Nei Menggu Jiefangyingzi Liao mu fajue jianbao' (Report on the discovery of a Liao tomb at Jiefangyingzi, Inner Mongolia), *Kaogu* (1979.4), 330–334 (early 11th century wooden model couch, table and chair). 'Jiangyin Bei Song Ruichang Xianjun Sun si niangzi mu' (The northern Song tomb of Fourth Lady Sun, Princess Ruichang at Jiangyin), *Wenwu* (1982.12), 28–35 (c.1050 model table and chair). Zhang Zengwu, 'Henan Linxian Chengguan Song mu qingli jianbao' (Report on a Song tomb at Chengguan, Lin county, Henan province), *Kaogu yu wenwu* (1982.5), 39–42 (c.1070 relief brickwork of an interior). 'Aohan qi Baitazi Liao mu' (A Liao tomb at Baitazi, Aohan Banner), *Kaogu* (1978.2), 119–121 (c.1081 model table). 'Luoyang Jianxi san zuo Songdai fang mu jie zhuan shi mu' (Three Song dynasty brick chamber tombs imitating wood construction at Jianxi, Luoyang), *Wenwu* (1983.8), 13–24 (c.1090 relief brickwork of interiors). Su Bo, *Baisha Song mu* (Song tombs at Baisha) (Peking, 1957) (11th century relief brickwork of interiors). 'Jiangsu Liyang Zhuze Bei Song Li Shan fu fu mu' (The northern Song tomb of Li Shan and his wife at Zhuze, Liyang county, Jiangsu province), *Wenwu* (1980.5), 34–44 (c.1090 ceramic models of sedan chairs). 'Datong Jindai Yan Deyuan mu fajue jianbao' (Report on the discovery of the Jin dynasty tomb of Yan Deyuan at Datong), *Wenwu* (1978.4), 1–13 (c.1190 wooden model tables, chair, couch and stands, fragmentary full-size tables). 'Shandong Gaotang Jindai Yu Yin mu fajue jianbao' (Report on the discovery of the Jin dynasty tomb of Yu Yin at Gaotang, Shandong province), *Wenwu* (1982.1), 49–51 (c.1195 murals of interiors). Ning Duxue & Zhong Changfa, 'Gansu Wuwei xijiao linchang Xixia mu qingli jianbao' (Report on a Xixia tomb at the Western Suburbs Plantation, Wuwei, Gansu province), *Kaogu yu wenwu* (1980.3), 63–66 (c.1200 model table and clothes racks). 'Jinan shiqu faxian Jin mu' (A Jin tomb discovered in the region of Jinan city), *Kaogu* (1979.6), 508–509, 507 (c. 1190 relief brickwork of an interior). 'Shanxi sheng Datong shi Yuandai Feng Daozhen, Wang Qing mu qingli jianbao' (Report on the Yuan dynasty tombs of Feng Daozhen and Wang Qing at Datong city, Shanxi province), *Wenwu cankao ziliao* (1962.10), (13th century wooden models of tables, chair and stands). Xiang Chunsong, 'Nei Menggu Chifeng shi Yuanbaoshan Yuandai bihua mu' (A Yuan dynasty tomb with murals at Yuanbaoshan, Chifeng city, Inner Mongolia), *Wenwu* (1983.5), 40–46 (13th century murals of interiors) 'Gansu Zhangxian Yuandai Wang Shixian jiazu muzang' (The Yuan dynasty burials of the family of Wang Shixian at Zhang county, Gansu province), *Wenwu* (1982.2), 1–18 (13th century ceramic table and model wooden clothes stand). 'Jiangsu Wujin Cunqian Nan Song mu qingli jiyao' (Report on the excavations of Southern Song tombs at Cunqian, Wujin, Jiangsu province), *Kaogu* (1986.3), 247–260 (13th century wooden model table and chair).

22 Chen Zengbi, 'Lun Handai wu zhuo', p.95.

23 *Song shi* ('The Song History'), Zhonghua shuju ed., 40 vols (Peking, 1977), XXV, 8932.

24 Fitzgerald, p.75 n.1.

25 Zhu Jiajin, 'Man tan yi deng ji qi chenshe ge shi' (On the Forms and Arrangement of Chairs and Stools), *Wenwu cankao ziliao* (1959.6), 3–7 (p.6).

26 Wang Shixiang, '*Lu Ban Jing . . .*', Part I, 61–62.'

27 Gao Lian, *Zun sheng ba jian* (1591 ed.), juan 8, p.16b.

28 Wen Zhenheng, pp.230 & 235.

29 Wang Shixiang, *Classic Chinese Furniture*, (London, 1986), no 50. Originally published in Chinese as *Ming shi jiaju zhenshang* ('An Appreciation of Ming Style Furniture') (Hong Kong, 1985).

30 Reyner Banham, *Theory and Design in the First Machine Age*, (London, 1960), p.191.

31 Robert Hatfield Ellsworth, *Chinese Furniture: Hardwood Examples of the Ming and Early Ch'ing Dynasties* (London and Glasgow, 1970), p. 271. Wang Shixiang, *Classic Chinese Furniture*, nos 44 & 45 defends the opposite view that Ming chairs did on occasion originally have solid wooden seats.

32 *Zhongguo gudian wenxue banhua Xuanji* ('Selected Woodblock Illustrations from Classical Chinese Literature'), edited by Fu Xihua, 2 vols (Peking, 1981), II, 687 & 696. Lu Yaohua, 'Zhejiang Jiaxing Ming Xiang shi mu' (The Ming tomb of a Mr Xiang at Jiaxing, Zhejiang), *Wenwu* (1982.8), 37–41 (p.41). Suzhou shi bowuguan, 'Suzhou Huqiu Wang Xijue mu qingli jilue' (Preliminary account of the excavation of the tomb of Wang Xijue at Huqiu, Suzhou), *Wenwu* (1975.3), 51–56 (p.56).

33 Chen Zengbi, 'Ming shi jiaju de gongneng yu zaoxing' (Function and Style in Ming Furniture), *Wenwu* (1981.3), 83–90 (p.84).

34 Wen Zhenheng, p.350.

35 *Zhongguo gudian wenxue banhua . . .* I. 130, 346 & II. 696.

36 Wang Shixiang, *Classic Chinese Furniture*, p.24.

37 *The Shanghai Museum of Art*, edited by Shen Zhiyu (New York, 1983).

38 *Fleur en fiole d'or* (*Jin Ping Mei cihua*), translated by André Lévy, 2 vols. (Paris, 1985), I, 481. *Xing shi yinyuan zhuan* 3 vols (Shanghai, 1980), I, 144 & I, 204.

39 Wang Yingkui, *Liunan sui bi*, Qingdai shiliao biji congkan (Peking, 1983), p.64. An imperial banquet with all the guests on stools is in Jonathan Spence, 'Ch'ing' in *Food in Chinese Culture; Anthropological and Historical Perspectives*, edited by K. C. Chang (New Haven and London, 1977), fig. 27.

40 Zhu Jiajin, '*Man tan yi deng . . .*', 4.

41 Wang Shixiang, '*Lu Ban Jing . . .*', I, 57.

42 *The Shanghai Museum of Art*, no 22.

43 *Zhongguo gudian wenxue banhua . . .* I, 194 & II, 687.

44 Shen Defu, *Wanli ye huo bian* (Unofficial Gleanings of the Wanli Period), Yuan Ming shiliao biji congkan, 3 vols (Peking, 1980), III, 663.

45 Xu Ke, *Qing bi lei chao*, (Shanghai, 1918) bi 88 'tai shi yi'.

46 Chen Zengbi, 'Tai shi yi kao' (On the 'Grand Tutor chair'), *Wenwu* (1983.8), 84–88.

47 Joan Hornby, 'China' in *Ethnographic Objects in the Royal Danish Kunstkammer 1650–1800*, edited by Bente Dam-Mikkelsen & Torben Lundbaek (Copenhagen, 1980), 155–219 (p.179).

48 *The Face of China, as seen by Photographers and Travelers 1860–1912*, preface by L. Carrington Goodrich, historical commentary by Nigel Cameron (New York, 1978) pp.21 & 97.

49 Craig Clunas, 'The Chinese Chair and the Danish Designer', *V & A Album 4* (London, 1985), 314–318.

50 Sir Harry Garner, *Chinese Lacquer* (London, 1979), p.138.

51 Shen Defu, II, 613.

52 'Kazakhs Presenting Tribute Horses', now in the Musée Guimet. *Europa und die Kaiser von China*, edited by Hendrik Budde, Christoph Muller-Hofstede & Gereon Sievernich, Berliner Festspiele (Berlin, 1985), no 12/21.

53 *Ming Qing renwu xiaoxianghua xuan/Portrait Paintings of the Ming and Qing Dynasties*, Nanjing Museum (Shanghai, 1979), nos 15, 18, 51 & 66.

54 *Fleur en fiole d'or*, I, 304.

55 'Sichuan Tongliangxian Mingdai shi guo mu' (Stone chambered tombs of the Ming dynasty at Tongliangxian, Sichuan) *Wenwu* (1983.2), 65–75 (p.75).

56 *15th Century Illustrated Chinese Primer: Hsin-pien Tui-hsiang Szu-yen* Facsimile reproduction with introduction and notes by L. Carrington Goodrich, second edition (Hong Kong, 1975), p.6b.

57 Zhu Jiajin, 'Man tan yi deng...', p.6.

58 *Zhongguo gudian wenxue banhua*...II, 844.

59 Wen Zhenheng, p.350.

60 Wen Zhenheng, pp. 226–228, Gao Lian, pp. 9b & 13a. Tu Long, p.1a.

61 Wang Shixiang, '*Lu Ban Jing*...', Part I, 59–61.

62 Acquisition no FE.2–1987. It is hoped this piece will form the object of a separate study.

63 Craig Clunas, 'A Chinese Bed for a European Trader', *Arts of Asia*, 13.6. (1983), 126–129 (p.129).

64 Li Yu, pp.28a–30a.

65 Zhu Jiajin, 'Man tan yi deng...', pl. 11.

66 H.F. Chow, *The familiar Trees of Hopei*, Peking Natural History Bulletin Handbook no 4 (Peking, 1934).

67 Rudolf P. Hommel, *China at Work, an Illustrated Record of the Primitive Industries of China's Masses, whose Life is Toil, and thus an Account of Chinese Civilisation* (New York, 1937), p.307.

68 Xie Zhaozhe, *Wu za zu* ('Five Collections of Miscellanea'), Guoxue zhenben wenku, 2 vols (Shanghai, 1935), II, 60.

69 *Report by Consul-General Hosie on the Province of the Ssu'chuan*, His Majesty's Stationery Office (London, 1904), pp. 55–56.

70 Zhu Jiajin, 'Yongzheng nian de jiaju zhizao kao', (The palace furniture workshop in the Yongzheng period), *GGBWYYK*, 1985.3, 105–111 (p.106).

71 Wu Tao, 'Qing Jiaqing nianjian Shaanxi mu gong he tie gong de qiyi' ('The Shaanxi iron and timber workers' uprising in the Jiaqing reign of the Qing period'), *Shixue yuekan* 1964, 8, 23–26.

72 William T. Rowe, *Hankow: Commerce and Society in a Chinese City 1796–1889* (Stanford, 1984), p.269.

73 Ellsworth, p.47. See also Edward H. Schafer, 'Rosewood, Dragon's Blood and Lac', *JAOS*, 77 (1955), 128–137.

74 Jean Gordon Lee, 'Chinese Furniture', *Philadelphia Museum Bulletin* (Winter, 1963).

75 Wang Shixiang, *Classic Chinese Furniture*, p.16.

76 F. Lewis Hinckley, *Directory of the Historic Cabinet Woods* (New York, 1960), p.118.

77 Sir Percival David, *Chinese Connoisseurship. The Ko Ku Yao Lun, The Essential Criteria of Antiquities* (London, 1971), p.154.

78 Huang Shengzeng. *Xi yang chao gong dian lu* ('Records on the Tribute of the Western Ocean'), annotated by Xie Fang (Peking, 1982), pp. 12 and 59.

79 Gu Jie, *Hai cha yu lu* ('A Record of a Raft on the Seas') quoted in Xie Guozhen, *Mingdai shehui jingji shiliao xuanbian* ('Selected Materials on Ming Social and Economic History'), 3 vols (Fuzhou, 1980), I, 271.

80 Xu Ke, *Qing hi lei chao, bi* 87, p.168.

81 Schafer, 132.

82 C.R. Boxer, *The Great Ship from Amacon: Annals of Macao and the Old Japan Trade*, 1555–1640 (Lisbon, 1959), p.184.

83 Sarasin Viraphol, *Tribute and Profit: Sino-Siamese Trade 1652–1853*, Harvard East Asian Monographs 76 (Harvard, 1977), pp.150–151.

84 India Office Records G/12/58.

85 Lu Jian, 'Tan Kangxi shiqi yu xi Ou de maoyi' ('Trade with Western Europe in the Kangxi period'), *Lishi dang'an* (1981.4), 113–116 (p.114).

86 Shi Zhilian, 'Ming Jiang Qianli kuan kan luodian hei qi zhihu he Ming zitan diao shiba xueshi changfang he' ('A

Ming ewer of black laquer inlaid with mother of pearl, bearing the signature Jiang Qianli and a Ming rectangular *zitan* box carved with the 'Eighteen Scholars'), *Wenwu* (1982.4), 70–73 (p.72).

87 Wang Shixiang, *Classic Chinese Furniture*, p.18.

88 *Shōsōin no shikkō* ('Lacquer in the Shosoin'), edited by Shōsōin jimusho (Tokyo, 1975), p.35.

89 *Zhongguo lidai huihua. Gugong bowuyuan zang hua ji I* ('Chinese Painting through the Ages. Chinese Painting in the Palace Muesum I') (Peking, 1978), pp.84–93.

90 'Fajue Ming Zhu Tan mu ji shi' ('An account of excavations at the Ming tomb of Zhu Tan'), *Wenwu* (1972.5), 25–36 (p.31).

91 David, p.106 and pp.148–149.

92 Wang Shixiang, *Classic Chinese Furniture*, p.14.

93 *Nihon no bukkyō o kizuita hitobito*, pl.180.

94 Wen Zhenheng, p.232.

95 e.g. Odilon Roche, *Les meubles de la Chine* (Paris, 1922), pl.28.

96 R.H. van Gulik, *The Lore of the Chinese Lute*, Monumenta Nipponica Monograph, 2nd edition (Tokyo & Rutland, 1968), pp.194–197.

97 Zhou Erxue, *Shang yan su xin lu* ('Records of Prolonged Gratification of the Simple Heart'), Meishu congshu chu ji dijiu ji (Shanghai, 1936), p.3b.

98 Shen Bang, *Wan shu za ji* ('Random Notes on the Administration of Wanping'), (Peking, 1980), p.155.

99 Zhou Shilin, pp.170a–170b.

100 Zhou Shilin, pp.251b–252a.

101 *Fleur en fiole d'or*, II, 1179.

102 Zhou Shilin, p.155b.

103 Zhou Shilin, p.18a.

104 Cao Xueqin and Gao E, *The Story of the Stone*, translated by David Hawkes and John Minford, 5 vols (London 1972–1986) 5, 121.

105 Chen Zengbi, 'Lun Handai wu zhuo', 95.

106 Sarah Ann Handler, *Pieces in Context; an Approach to the Study of Chinese Domestic Furniture through an Analysis of Ming Dynasty Domestic Hardwood Examples in Kansas City* (Unpublished Ph.D. thesis, University of Kansas, 1983), p.62.

107 George Kubler, *The Shape of Time, Remarks on the History of Things* (New Haven and London, 1962), p.70.

108 Wang Shixiang, *Classic Chinese Furniture*, p. 19, where the English terminology used for *zhuo* and *an* is 'waisted' and 'waistless'.

109 *15th Century Illustrated Chinese Primer*, p.3a.

110 Wang Shixiang, 'Lu Ban Jing . . .', Part II, 76.

111 *Zhongguo gudian wenxue banhua xuanji*, I, 211, 272, II 198.

112 *Zhongguo gudian wenxue banhua xuanji*, I, 140, 199, p.298, p.335, II, p.675.

113 *Xing shi yin yuan zhuan*, I. 36.

114 'Suzhou Huqiu Wang Xijue mu', p.56.

115 Gustav Ecke, *Chinese Domestic Furniture*, facsimile of the 1944 Peking first edition (Rutland and Tokyo, 1963), no 36 is the same table before alteration.

116 Jessica Rawson, *Chinese Ornament; the Lotus and the Dragon* (London, 1984), pp. 132–138.

117 Wang Shixiang, 'Lu Ban Jing . . .', I, 65.

118 *Zhongguo gudian wenxue banhua xuanji*, I, 280, II, 626.

119 *The Voyage of John Huyghen van Linschoten to the East Indies* edited by Arthur Cooke Burnell and P. A. Tiele, Hakluyt Society, 2 vols (London, 1885), I, 143. Linschoten did not reach China himself, but many of his details about the empire are trustworthy.

120 *Xing shi yin yuan zhuan* I, 73.

121 Wang Shixiang, 'Shuyao he tuosai-manhua gudai jiaju he jianzhu de guanxi' (The shuyao and the tuosai-a note on the relationship between ancient furniure and architecture), *Wenwu*, 1982, 1, 78–80.

122 Wang Shixiang, *Classic Chinese Furniture*, p.26.

123 Published as Ecke, no. 33.

124 *Zhongguo gudian wenxue banhua xuanji*, II, 587, 844. Levy, *Fleur en fiole d'or*, I, 137.

125 Wen Zhenheng, p.233.

126 Wen Zhenheng, p.231.

127 Zhang Dai, *Tao an meng yi* (Dream Recollections from Joyous Hermitage), Xi hu shu she ed. (Hangzhou, 1982), *juan* 6, p.80.

128 Ecke, no. 66.

129 Zhou Erxue, p.3b.

130 Zhu Jiajin, 'Yongzheng nian de jiaju zhizao kao' ('The palace furniture workshop in the Yongzheng period'), *GGBWYYK*, 1985.3, 105–111 (p.106).

131 Wang Shixiang, 'Lu Ban Jing', I, 65.

132 Wne Zhenheng, pp.233–234.

133 James Cahill, *Parting at the Shore. Chinese Painting of the Early and Middle Ming Dynasty, 1368–1580* (New York and Tokyo, 1978), colour plate 2.

134 Frederick W. Mote, 'Yüan and Ming' in *Food in Chinese Culture*, pp. 193–257 (p.246).

135 I am grateful to John Bornhoft for this suggestion.

136 L. Reidemeister, 'Der Grosse Kürfurst und Friedrich III als Sammler Ostasiatische Kunst. Wiederentdeckungen aus der Brandenburgisch-Preussischen Kuntskammer'. *Ostasiatische Zeitschrift* N. F. 8 (1932), 175–188 (p.183).

137 Ellsworth, p.63 and p.66.

138 Marcel Bernanose, *Les arts decoratifs au Tonkin* (Paris, 1922), pls. 34 and 35.

139 *Chinese Furniture*, notes prepared by William Drummond, The Sackler Collections, Series 13, Lecture 1 (New York, 1969), 13–1–1.

140 Wang Ao, *Gusu zhi*, 1539 ed, Zhongguo shixue congshu 31, 2 vols (Taibei, 1965), I, 212.

141 Li Yu, p.26b.

142 Bian Xiaoxuan, 'Tangdai Yangzhou shougongye yu chutu wenwu' ('Handicrafts in Yangzhou under the Tang dynasty in the light of excavated pieces'), *Wenwu*, 1979.9, 31–37 (p.36).

143 Gu Lu, *Tong qiao yi zhuo lu* ('Leaning on the Table by Paulonia Bridge'), Shanghai guji chubanshe ed. (Shanghai, 1980), p.153.

144 Wen Zhenheng, p.235.

145 Robert Fortune, *Three Years Wanderings in the Northern Provinces of China* (London, 1847), p.89.

146 Wen Zhenheng, pp.235, 240, 241.

147 *Fleur en fiole d'or*, I, 128 & II, 1206.

148 *Guanyu Jiangning zhizao Cao jia dang'an shiliao* (Archival material on the Cao family Superintendents of the Jiangning Weaving Office), edited by Gugong Bowuyuan Ming Qing dang'an bu (Peking, 1975), pp.4–5.

149 *Ming shi* ('The Ming History'), Zhonghua shuju ed., 28 vols (Peking, 1974), VI, 1819.

150 Liu Wanchun (*jinshi* of 1616), *Shou guan man lu* ('An Unofficial Account of Official Life'), quoted in Xie Guozhen III, 293.

151 Zhu Jiajin, 'Yongzheng nian de jiaju zhizao kao (xu)' ('The palace furniture workshop in the Yongzheng period; Park II'), *GGBWYYK*, 1985.4, 79–87 (p.86).

152 Li Yu, p.31a.

153 C.R. Boxer, *South China in the Sixteenth Century*, Hakluyt Society (London, 1953), pp.106 & 125.

154 George N. Kates, *Chinese Household Furniture* (New York, 1948), p.5.

155 Hong Huanchun, 'Ming Qing Suzhou diqu zibenzhuyi mengya chubu kaocha'. (A preliminary investigation of the sprouts of capitalism in the Suzhou region during the Ming and Qing) in *Ming Qing zibenzhuyi mengya yanjiu lunwen ji* (Collected Essays on Research into the Sprouts of Capitalism in the Ming and Qing), edited by Liu Baihan and Wang Jieyun (Shanghai, 1981), pp.399–449 (406–410).

156 John Steward Burgess, *The Guilds of Peking*, Studies in History, Economics and Public Law, edited by the Faculty of Political Science of Columbia University, no 308 (New York, 1928), p.59.

157 Burgess, pp.113, 140, 165 & 258.

158 Eugene Cooper, pp.450–454.

159 Donald R. De Glopper, 'Doing Business in Lukang', in *Economic Organization in Chinese Society*, Studies in Chinese Society (Stanford, 1972), 297–326 (pp.229–300).

160 *Xing shi yin yuan zhuan*, I, 133.

161 Philip D. Zimmerman, 'Workmanship as Evidence: a Model for Object Study', *Winterthur Portfolio*, 16 (1981), 283–307 (310–304).

162 Wang Shixiang, *Classic Chinese Furniture*, p.27.

163 Hu Wenyan, 'Ming shi jiaju de zhuangshi' (The decoration of Ming-style furniture), *Wenwu*, 1985.1, 80–82 (p.82) gives example of some surviving carpenters' mnemonies.

164 H.A. Giles, 'Thousand Character Numerals Used by Artisans', *Journal of the Royal Asiatic Society, China Branch*, 20 (1885), 279.

165 Zhu Jiajin, 'Yongzheng nian . . . (xu)', p.86.

166 Richard Ollard, *Pepys, a Biography* (London, 1974), p.107.

167 Li Yu, pp.25a–26b.

168 George A. Kennedy, 'Chu Yu-chiao' in *Eminent Chinese of the Ch'ing Period*, edited by Arthur W. Hummel (Washington, 1943), p.190.

169 From a series of poems on crafts, *Ri yong su zi* in *Pu Songling ji* (Collected Works of Pu Songling), 2 vols, Zhonghua shuju (Peking, 1962), I, 742. I am grateful to Alan Barr for this reference.

170 Joseph Needham, *Science and Civilisation in China, Volume 4: Physics and Physical Technology, Part II: Mechanical Engineering* (Cambridge, 1965), p.54.

171 Hommel, pp.224–257 concern tools for woodworking.

172 Chen Rongsheng, *Mu gong* (Woodworking), second edition (Canton, 1979), pp.14–39.

173 *15th Century Illustrated Chinese Primer*, p.3b.

174 Wang Shixiang, 'Lu Ban jing . . .', Part I, 55.

175 David Pye, *The Nature and Art of Workmanship* (Cambridge, 1968), p18.

176 Pak Yŏng-gyu, *Han'guk ui mok kagu* (Wooden Furniture of Korea) (Seoul, 1982), pp.336–351 shows the complete toolkit of the Korean cabinetmaker.

177 Wang Shixiang, 'Lu Ban jing . . .', Part I, 55.

178 *Chinese Ivories from the Shang to the Qing*, edited by William Watson, The Oriental Ceramic Society (London, 1984), p.195.

179 Ju Zhai, 'Go chi kao' (On ancient footrules), *Wenwu cankao ziliao* 1957.3, 25–28.

180 Garner, *Chinese Lacquer*, p.92.

181 British Museum OA.1937–7–16.6.12(70).

182 Yu Xin, 'Jing fu', quoted in *Pei wen yun fu*, Taiwan shangwu yinshuguan ed., 7 vols, V, 4229.

183 Zhou Mi, *Gui xing za zhi*, quoted in *Pei wen yun fu*, V, 4229.

184 Penelope Eames, 'Medieval Furniture in England, France and the Netherlands from the Twelfth to the Fifteenth Century', *Furniture History*, 12 (1977), 1–301 (pls. 22–26).

185 Li Yu, p.25b.

186 Wang Shixiang, 'Lu Ban jing . . .', Part I, 65.

187 Wang Shixiang, *Classic Chinese Furniture*, p.32.

188 E. Fuhrmann, *China. Erster Teil: Das Land der Mitte*, Geist Kunst und Leben Asiens IV, edited by Karl With (Hagen, 1921) p.133.

189 Wen Zhenheng, pp.240–341.

190 Wang Shixiang, *Classic Chinese Furniture*, p.30.

191 Wang Shixiang, 'Lu Ban jing . . .', Part II, 83.

192 *15th Century Illustrated Chinese Primer*, p.3a.

193 *15th Century Illustrated Chinese Primer*, p.3a.

194 Li Yu, p.30a.

195 *Gugong bowuyuan zang gongyipin xuan* ('Selected Handicrafts in the Collection of the Palace Museum') (Peking, 1974), no 45.

196 Wen Zhenheng, p.238.

197 Gao Lian, p.36a.

198 Wen Zhenheng, p.240.

199 Wang Shixiang, 'Lu ban jing . . .', Part I, 59.

200 Yang Hao, 'Qing chu Wu Liuqi mu ji qi xunzang yiwu' ('The Early Qing Tomb of Wu Liuqi and its Funerary Artefacts') *Wenwu* (1982.2), 39–43 (pl. 6).

201 Verity Wilson, *Chinese Dress*, Victoria and Albert Museum Far Eastern Series (London, 1986), p.92.

202 C.R. Boxer, *South China in the Sixteenth Century*, p.106.

203 *Ju jia bi yong shi lei quan ji* ('A Complete Collection of Necessary Matters Ordered for the Householder'), Wanli ed., 10 juan, I, p.6b.

204 Wang Shixiang, *Classic Chinese Furniture*, pp.30–31.

205 Gao Lian, p.37a.

206 Inv. nos 51.100.1 & 51.100.2.

207 *Xing shi yin yuan zhuan*, I, 128.

208 Sören Edgren et al., *Chinese Rare Books in American Collections*, China House Gallery (New York, 1984), pp.114–115.

209 Margaret Medley, 'Lacquered Furniture' in *Lacquerwork in Asia and Beyond*, edited by William Watson, Percival David Foundation Colloquies on Art and Archaeology in Asia No. 11 (London 1982), pp.70–84 (p.74).

210 Lee Yu-kuan, *Oriental Lacquer Art* (New York/Tokyo, 1972), pp.339–340.

211 Wang Shixiang, 'Lu Ban jing . . .', Part I, 63.

212 Li Yu, p.26b.

213 Wen Zhenheng, pp.243–244.

214 *Modern Chairs (1918–1970)*, Whitechapel Art Gallery (London, 1970), pp.26–28.

215 Hans Wegner, 'Furniture' in *Design since 1949*, edited by Kathryn B. Hiesinger and George H. Marcus, Philadelphia Museum of Art (Philadelphia, 1983), pp.118–120.

216 E.H. Gombrich, *A Sense of Order, a study in the psychology of decorative art* (London, 1979), pp.59–61.

217 Wang Shixiang, 'Xiaoshan Zhu shi jiu zang zhengui jiaju ji lue' ('An Account of the Fine Furniture Collection of the Zhu Family of Xiaoshan'), *Wenwu* 1984.10, 53–58 (p.58).

218 Roche, pp.vi–vii.

219 Herbert Cescinsky, *Chinese Furniture* (London, 1922), pp.9–16.

220 Marcel Dupont, *Les meubles de la Chine; deuxieme serie* (Paris, 1927), pp.v–viii.

221 'Chinese Furnishings dominate this charming Shanghai Home', *Arts and Decoration*, 37 (May, 1932), 18–19: 'Antiques in Domestic Settings', *Antiques*, 33 (March, 1938), 134–135: 'At Home in a Royal Chinese Palace', *Arts and Decoration*, 49 (March, 1939), 19.

222 'Functionalism in Antique Chinese Furniture', *Antiques*, 38 (1940), 33.

223 John C. Ferguson, *Survey of Chinese Art* (Shanghai, 1940), pp.110–112.

224 Ecke, p.1 & pp.28–33.

225 'Chinese Furniture', *Baltimore Museum of Art News*, (June, 1946), 1–2 (p.1).

226 George Kates, *Chinese Household Furniture* (New York, 1948), pp.3, 18 and 58.

227 John D. Morse, 'Dynasty Furniture', *American Artist*, 19 (May, 1955) pp.40–41 & 70–72.

228 Michel Beurdeley, *Chinese Furniture* (Tokyo, New York and San Francisco, 1979).

229 Handler, pp.61 & 94.

Index